Across the Curriculum

with

Favorite Authors

Eric Carle

Written by John and Patty Carratello

Illustrated by Cheryl Buhler, Sue Fullam and Keith Vasconcelles

The authors wish to thank Barbara Pelham for her valuable help.

Teacher Created Materials, Inc.
P.O. Box 1040
Huntington Beach, CA 92647
©1992 Teacher Created Materials, Inc.
Made in U.S.A.

ISBN 1-55734-451-5

Table of Contents

Introduction

Our teaching is enriched daily by the wealth of outstanding authors who give us words and pictures to engage, motivate, and inspire our students. Through these authors, our students become acquainted with worlds and ideas beyond their own and emerge to be more aware, active, and enthusiastic readers.

In this author series, one author is spotlighted in each resource book. Teachers and students have the opportunity to participate in an in-depth study of each author's works and style.

In this book you will find:

- Sample lesson plans for the classroom teacher

- Biographical information for a closer look at the author's life, style, motivations, and place in literary history

- Ways to design a classroom to generate interest in the author

- In-depth, cross-curricular lessons on individual books, according to this format:
  — *Book Summaries*
  — *Before Reading the Book* ideas
  — *While Reading the Book* ideas
  — *After Reading the Book* ideas

- A culminating activity which will serve to showcase the students' involvement with the author

- Assessment tools, structured to stimulate critical thinking skills

- A bibliography and answer key

We are confident the author approach to studying literature will be a satisfying experience for you and your students!

Sample Lesson Plans

These lessons are just a suggested guide. You may find that some books and related activities can fill a week or two!

Preparation

- Preview the books and activities suggested in this resource.
- Collect the Eric Carle books you want to use. (pages 2 and 111)
- Create a classroom environment to stimulate an interest in Eric Carle. (page 9)

Lesson 1

- Present biographical information on Eric Carle. (page 7)
- Distribute Eric Carle's picture for a class art project. (page 6) You may suggest a number of ways students can use his picture. Here are just a few:

  - ☆ Color with crayons, chalk, or marker.
  - ☆ Paint with available painting materials.
  - ☆ Make a mosaic with tiny pieces of construction paper.
  - ☆ Trace on tracing paper and overlay on an excerpt from one of his books.
  - ☆ Use as the background for tissue paper collage.

- Discuss and demonstrate the art technique that has brought Eric Carle much fame. (page 8)
- Give the students an opportunity to try one of his art techniques.

Lesson 2 through Lesson 14, an overview

- Present the "Before Reading the Book" activities you find most appropriate for your students and curriculum.
- Be sure to practice reading the book aloud before you present it to your students.
- During your class reading, monitor your students' ability to listen actively. Watch for physical clues, as well as questions, answers, and comments that are generated by active student involvement.
- Present appropriate "While Reading the Book" activities.
- Extend the book by encouraging "After Reading the Book" activities that are of interest to your students.

Sample Lesson Plans

Lesson 2, an elaboration *Do You Want to Be My Friend?*

- Present any number of "Before Reading the Book" activities for *Do You Want to Be My Friend?*. This book is particularly good for the first week of school, when so many children want to find and be friends.

- While reading the book, discuss the types of friends a mouse might have, and speculate what kind of animal belongs to each tail. At this time, make the "Guess Who?" tail books suggested on page 10.

- After reading the book, draw pictures, write stories, and play games about friendships. (page 10)

Lesson 15

- Prepare students for the Culminating Activity on pages 98 to 104.
- Share ideas for murals. (pages 98 and 99)
- Review Eric Carle books you have studied.
- Prepare mural background. (page 100)
- Choose designs. Many are provided in this resource book.
- Evaluate mural with personalized figures. (page 103)
- Create Eric Carle books using graduated paper sizes. (page 104)

Lesson 16

- Choose the assessments that are appropriate for your students' interest and ability level.

- When conducting the application assessment suggested on page 107, you may find that it can be extended into a week's lesson. Students usually take great interest and pride in developing their own lessons for the study of a book.

- If this is successful, encourage them to develop lessons for other Eric Carle books working in small groups. The entire class can then enjoy many more books by the author, and the students have personalized their learning!

Lesson 17

- Visit the library. Encourage students to read more books written and/or illustrated by Eric Carle. (page 111)

Eric Carle

About the Author

Eric Carle was born on June 25, 1929 in Syracuse, New York to German-American parents. His interest in art began at an early age. He remembered painting on large sheets of paper with bright colors and wide brushes in kindergarten. His delight with creating bright and colorful illustrations might have begun with that happy kindergarten experience.

When he was just beginning first grade, Eric's family moved to Stuttgart, Germany because of the encouragement of his paternal grandmother. Eric dealt with the struggle of adapting to harsh conditions in his new school, learning a new language, and overcoming his homesickness. In *Famous Children's Authors*, he said, "Often I wished that a bridge could be built from Germany to America so I could get back home." But, soon he made new friends, began to speak German fluently, was encouraged in his drawing by an art teacher, and was surrounded by loving relatives.

While in Germany, Eric Carle witnessed the beginnings of open anti-Semitism and World War II. At the outbreak of the war, Eric's father was drafted into the German army and was gone for eight years, a part of which was spent as a prisoner of war in Russia. All the while he was gone, Eric deeply missed him. When Allied forces began to attack Stuttgart, townspeople dug tunnels where they could take shelter from the air raids. Carle and many other young children were sent to the safety of a small town in southwestern Germany. After the war, when the family was finally reunited, Carle's father was a changed man. Carle longed for the happiness and closeness they had once had, remembering the times he had spent exploring and learning a love of nature from his father. The son had to settle for the memories.

Carle studied art with Professor Ernst Schneidler at the Akademie der bildenden Kuenste and easily found work in his field, beginning with designing posters for a local American information center. After gaining experience and confidence, he returned to the United States to work.

After working for years as a designer and art director, Eric Carle decided to become a free-lance artist. An interest in children's literature blossomed when he agreed to illustrate books written by Bill Martin. Encountering this stimulating work for young children awakened the child in him that had been lost in wartime Germany. In a *Something about the Author* Autobiography Series essay, Carle revealed, "The child inside me—who had been so suddenly and sharply uprooted and repressed—was beginning to come joyfully back to life."

This joy is evident in Carle's books in the bold, bright colors, original art techniques, lively animals, playful details, and clever paper engineering. A cricket chirps as you turn the last page in *The Very Quiet Cricket*. A child's finger can trace the raised spider's web in *The Very Busy Spider*. A caterpillar eats away holes in different types of food on the pages of *The Very Hungry Caterpillar*. Pages grow in size as do the animals encountered by a grouchy insect in *The Grouchy Ladybug*. These are just a few of the many examples of Carle's desire to make his books transitions from toys to literature, and to make reading and learning fun. In *Books for Your Children*, Carle explains, "I would like to make childhood something special and joyous, something that the child does not want to get over with fast, something that immunizes him from such warnings as 'time to grow up,' 'be mature,' and 'don't act like a child.'" Eric Carle has done just that, as his many awards and honors prove.

Tissue Paper Collage

Eric Carle revolutionized illustration in children's books with his bold art techniques and paper engineering. One of the methods bringing him fame is the use of tissue paper collage. This technique, often used by Eric Carle to illustrate his books for children, is an exciting and easy method for children to use to incorporate vivid blendings of color into their artwork.

Materials: a variety of colored art tissue paper; brushes of various widths; containers of thinned white glue or laundry starch; scissors; something to sketch with; white or light-colored construction paper for background; smocks (may be old shirts buttoned backwards); newspaper (to cover tables); place for drying papers.

Begin by tearing a few small pieces of tissue of different colors and overlapping them on a small piece of white construction paper. Brush the top surfaces with starch. The liquid penetrates the thin paper, blends the colors, and bonds the tissue to the background sheet. Light colors on top of dark colors almost disappear, so it is best to start with light colors first.

The brush will often pick up color from the tissue and spread it to the background paper. This can become part of the design or can be avoided by stopping the brush before it reaches the background paper. Subtle shadings can be obtained by overlapping pieces of the same color. Brilliant combinations and contrasts appear when different colors overlap.

To add subject matter, sketch an outline or work without one to make planned shapes. Tissue can be cut to a sharp edge or torn for a softer look. Many small pieces may be combined to fill in an outline.

Let the tissue collages dry thoroughly before adding details and textures as Eric Carle does. Add line with crayons, pastels, and markers, and apply paint with brushes, sponges, and a variety of fabrics, objects, and gadgets. Paint may be brushed on an object such as an empty spool, or the object may be tapped on a sponge saturated with paint and then applied to the collage. Margarine tub lids are useful as trays to hold sponges used as paint pads. Besides spools, some interesting objects for printing are vegetables, bottle caps, plastic forks, erasers, lace, and tracing wheels. Begin a class collection of printing objects.

Setting Up for Eric Carle

Students will be eager to learn about Eric Carle and his work in a classroom that is bright and lively with his books and art techniques.

Be sure that you have allowed plenty of room for the display of Eric Carle projects. A large bulletin board area would provide an excellent showcase. A wire strung across the classroom can serve as a place to clip up drying artwork as well as a display area for finished work. Projects can also hang from strings on the ceiling. You can even display a project a day on your desk or podium!

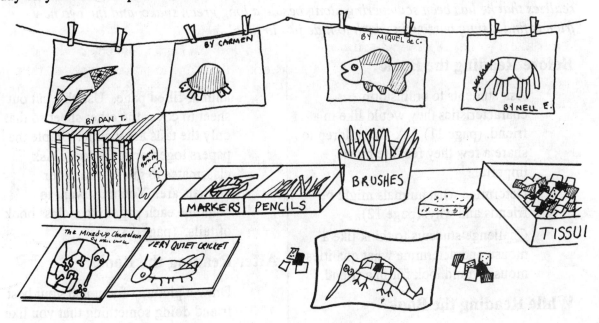

A center for storage of art supplies where children can easily reach materials will make setting up for various projects easier. Here are some ideas:

- a tub or box for smocks or paintshirts
- a supply of different sizes of paper on a low shelf
- a box for tissue paper scraps
- a tall plastic container for brushes that can be filled with water so brushes can be soaked before rinsing
- plastic margarine tubs for starch or glue mixtures (One for every two students works well.)
- containers of pencils, pens, markers, and crayons
- a basket for scissors
- newspapers
- a roll of paper towels
- wipe cloths from the "rag bag"
- sponges for cleanup

Do You Want To Be My Friend?
by Eric Carle
Thomas Y. Crowell, 1971
Available in Canada from Harper Collins, Canada

Summary

A lonely little mouse looks for a friend as he scampers along. He sees a tail and follows it to its owner, only to discover an animal who is not interested in friendship with a mouse. He chases tail after tail until he finds another little mouse who wants to be his friend. He realizes that he has been scampering along beside a long green snake, and the two new friends find a snug burrow in which to hide just in time!

Before Reading the Book

- Ask students to brainstorm characteristics they would like in a friend. (page 11) Ask the children to share a few they feel are most important.
- Determine what animals might be friends and why. (page 12)
- Challenge students to think like a mouse and determine what qualities a mouse would look for in a friend.

While Reading the Book

- Before turning each page, see if students can guess which animals will come next, using only the tails as clues.
- Try to determine if each of the encountered animals will be a good friend for the lonely mouse. Be sure your students give reasons.
- Cut out magazine pictures of animals with tails and glue them onto a piece of construction paper. On a separate, same-size piece of paper, cut holes to match where the tails are on the animal-filled page. Use this cut out sheet to cover the other sheet so that only the tails are visible. Staple the papers together at the top. Ask classmates to guess what your animals are. You may want to combine each page into a class book of tails. (page 13)

After Reading the Book

- Draw a picture of you and your best friend doing something that you like to do together. (page 14)
- Write a story about a friend you have or would like to have.
- Play a "friendship" guessing game. One child sits in the middle of a class circle and gives three clues to describe one of his or her friends. ("My friend has freckles.") The rest of the class tries to guess the friend's identity from the clues. Ask for guesses after each hint. Give the most general hint first and the most specific hint last. (page 15)

Friends

Quickly write as many characteristics of friends as you can. Here are a few examples to get you started.

kind   *honest*

funny   *good bike rider*

Write in the space below until your teacher tells you to stop.

Circle the two characteristics you think are most important. List them below and explain why they are important to you.

1. _____ is important in a friend because

_____

_____

2. _____ is important in a friend because

_____

_____

Could These Animals Be Friends?

Draw a line from each animal on the left to the animal on the right that could be its friend. Be ready to give reasons for the choices you have made. Choose one of your combinations and write or tell a story about their friendship.

Guess the Animals

1. Cut pictures of animals with tails from magazines, or draw your own animal pictures. Be sure the tail can be easily seen.

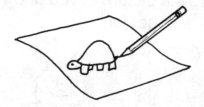

2. Paste or glue the pictures on a sheet of construction paper. Save a margin on the left side for book binding.

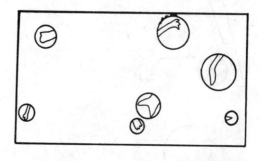

3. Cut holes in a cover sheet so that only the tails of the animals are visible. Or, make flaps to cover all but the animals' tails. This flap can be glued in place and lifted up to reveal the hidden animal.

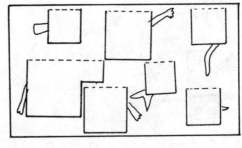

4. Put pages together to make a class book.

My Best Friend

Draw a picture of you and your best friend doing something that you like to do together.

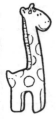

My best friend is _____

We like to _____

Guess Who?

Teacher: Give a slip to each child. Ask him or her to write the name of someone in the class on the top line. Then each child writes three clues that describe the person. The first clues should not narrow down the field too quickly, so encourage the children to write general clues first, and get very specific on the third. Model a set of clues for the students first.

Clue 1: "She has long hair."
Clue 2: "You can always find her on the swings at recess."
Clue 3: "She wears glasses for reading time."

Have the students take turns guessing "mystery friends."

Mystery Friend:	**Mystery Friend:**
Clue #1	Clue #1
Clue #2	Clue #2
Clue #3	Clue #3

The Secret Birthday Message

by Eric Carle
Harper & Row, 1986
Available in Canada from Harper Collins, Canada

Summary

On the eve of his birthday, Tim discovers an envelope that has been tucked under his pillow. In it is a secret message that uses shapes to give him directions for finding his birthday present!

Before Reading the Book

- Introduce and/or review the shapes used in the story. (pages 18 to 21)
- Find geometrical shapes in your classroom, such as a square cupboard, a rectangular door, a circular clock, an oval sink, a triangular picture, the stars on the flag, etc.
- Read *Circles, Triangles, and Squares* by Tana Hoban (Macmillan, 1974) and *Listen To a Shape* by Marcia Brown (Franklin Watts, 1979). See the shapes they have found in everyday things.

While Reading the Book

- Invite students to guess what is behind each shape before you turn the page. See if they can guess the birthday present!

- Enjoy geometrically shaped cookies as you read the book. Before they are eaten, each shape must be correctly identified.

- Encourage students to answer questions such as these:

   "Did Tim have fun hunting for his present? Would you?"

   "Did Tim go back the same way he came? Why?"

   "Who gave Tim the present? What are some clues?"

After Reading the Book

- Discuss special presents students have received or given.
- Write or verbalize the directions Tim will need to take to retrace his steps back to his bedroom.
- Encourage students to write their own secret messages using shapes to give directions.
- Ask students to go on a shape hunt in one or more rooms of their houses. They are to look for and report on matches between shapes they have learned and things in their homes.
- Make stencils (page 17). Use these stencils to make many projects, including your own shape books! (page 17)

Make Your Own Shape Books

Make Stencils and Patterns

Use tagboard or other heavy paper to make stencil or pattern shapes. These can be used for many projects, including making shape books! Reproduce the patterns on pages 18 to 21 onto tagboard and cut out. Or, follow the directions below.

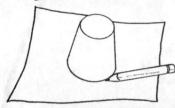  

1. Use an object to draw the outline of a shape on tag.
2. Cut the shape out of the tag. Try to keep your edges smooth.
3. Use your stencil or pattern to draw shapes.

Shape Flap Book

1. Think of a message that has four (or any number you choose) words, phrases or sentences.
2. Choose four (or the number chosen) shapes from pages 18 - 22. Make stencils or patterns for these shapes (see above) and trace them onto various colors of construction paper. Cut out these shapes.
3. Trace the shapes again onto a sheet of light-colored paper. Write your message inside these shapes (one part per shape).
4. Glue an edge of each cut out shape over its matching shape so that it can be lifted to read the message underneath.
5. Provide your readers with a "map" so that they know the order in which to read the message.

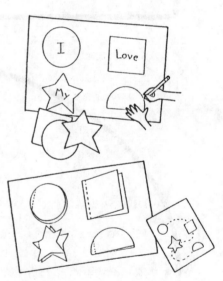

Shape-a-Page Book

1. Choose stencils or patterns made from the shapes on pages 18-20 to trace and cut out from various colored construction paper.
2. Glue these shapes at the top of sheets of light-colored paper.
3. Cut around the top edges of the shapes.
4. Write your story below the shapes.
5. Add tissue paper collage, paint, and/or other details to the shapes.
6. Make a cover and assemble your pages into a book.

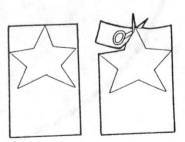

Shape Patterns

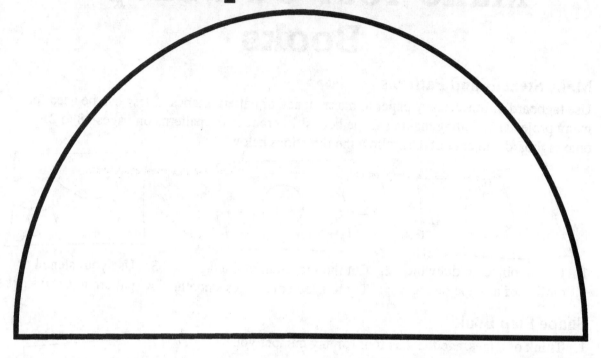

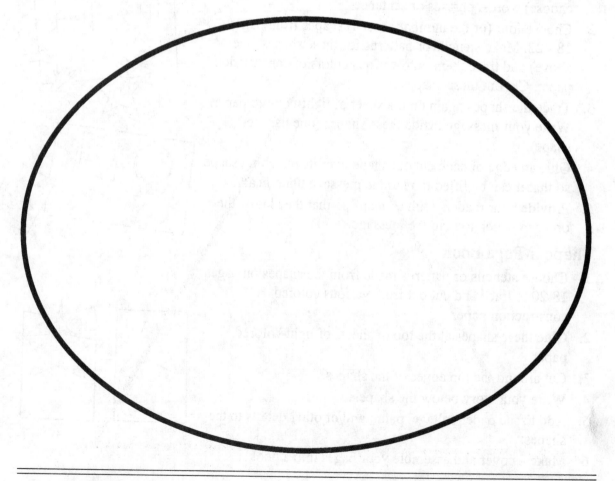

Shape Patterns *(cont.)*

Shape Patterns *(cont.)*

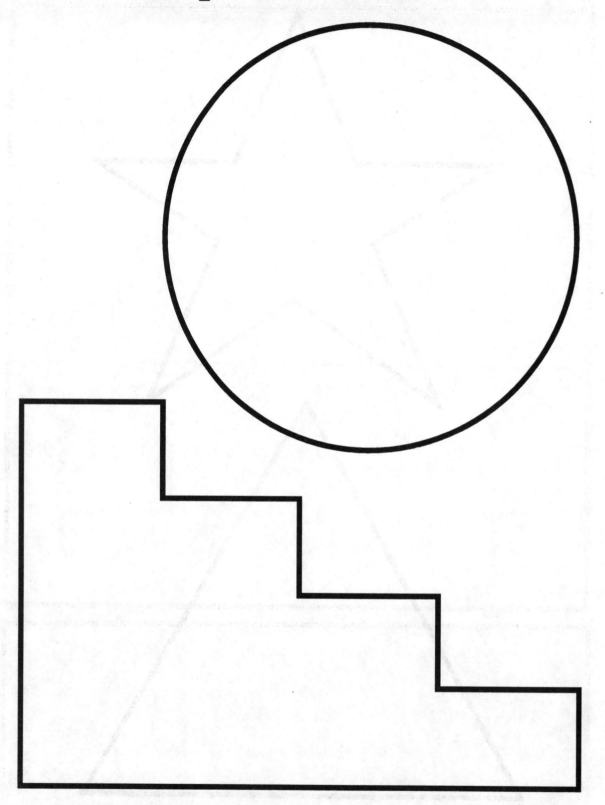

Shape Patterns *(cont.)*

Brown Bear, Brown Bear, What Do You See?

by Bill Martin, Jr. with pictures by Eric Carle
Henry Holt & Co., 1983

Available in Canada from Fitzhenry & Whitside, Ltd.

Summary

"What do you see?" is the question asked of each character in this story. In charming pictures and simple repetitive text, we find out!

Before Reading the Book

- Practice patterned response. You might sing a call-response song or play a call-response game. You might lead a mathematics lesson which requires a comprehension of patterns, such as triangle, circle, circle, triangle, circle, _____.

- Give students graph paper and invite them to design their own patterns.

- Brainstorm a list of things a brown bear might see.

While Reading the Book

- Ask students to anticipate what each animal will see.

- After each animal speaks, before you turn the page, ask the students to draw what they think the animal just mentioned will look like.

- Sequence the order of animals and people used in the book. (page 23) Assign parts for a dramatic reading of the story.

After Reading the Book

- Cut apart sentence strips and sequence the story (pages 24 and 25). Help students retell the story by making their own Brown Bear books using the sentence strips and the patterns provided on pages 24 to 31.

- Use the patterns on pages 26 to 31 for art projects. You may want to paint the bear, apply tissue paper collage to the redbird, scissor-curl black construction paper for the sheep, mosaic the goldfish, cotton ball the dog, or use crayons!

- Use the pattern of the story to make original stories about any subject that interests your students.

    "Dark cloud, dark cloud, What do you see?"
    "I see a rain storm coming from me."
    "Rain storm, rain storm, What do you see?"
    "I see a rainbow just past that tree."

- Practice patterned reading and responding. There are quite a few pattern books that appeal to a variety of ages. Here are several that have been used successfully: *There Was an Old Lady Who Swallowed a Fly* illustrated by Pam Adams, (Child's Play, 1989); *Drummer Hoff* by Barbara Emberly (Simon and Schuster, 1967); *The Napping House* by Audrey Wood (HBJ, 1984).

- Read *Polar Bear, Polar Bear, What Do You Hear?* written by Bill Martin, Jr. with pictures by Eric Carle. (Henry Holt and Company, 1991)

Trace the Pattern!

Start at the star and find the animals in the order told in *Brown Bear, Brown Bear, What Do You See?*

Sentence Strips

"Brown Bear, Brown Bear, What do you see?"

"I see a redbird looking at me."

"Redbird, redbird, What do you see?"

"I see a yellow duck looking at me."

"Yellow duck, yellow duck, What do you see?"

"I see a blue horse looking at me."

"Blue horse, blue horse, What do you see?"

"I see a green frog looking at me."

"Green frog, green frog, What do you see?"

"I see a purple cat looking at me."

"Purple cat, purple cat, What do you see?"

"I see a white dog looking at me."

"White dog, white dog, What do you see?"

"I see a black sheep looking at me."

"Black sheep, black sheep, What do you see?"

"I see a goldfish looking at me."

"Goldfish, goldfish, What do you see?"

"I see a mother looking at me."

"Mother, mother, What do you see?"

"I see beautiful children looking at me."

"Children, children, What do you see?"

"We see a brown bear,	a redbird,	a yellow duck,

a blue horse,	a green frog,	a purple cat,	a white dog,

a black sheep,	a goldfish,	and a mother looking at us."

"That's what we see."

Brown Bear and Redbird Patterns

Yellow Duck and Blue Horse Patterns

Green Frog and Purple Cat Patterns

White Dog and Black Sheep
Patterns

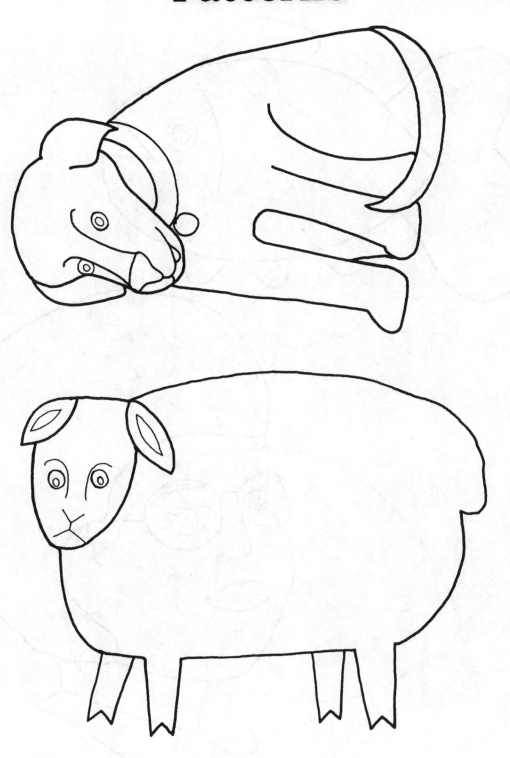

Goldfish and Mother
Patterns

Beautiful Children Patterns

The Very Hungry Caterpillar

by Eric Carle
Philomel, 1969
Available in Canada, UK, and Australia from Scholastic

Summary

As a tiny and very hungry caterpillar hatches from a little white egg on a leaf, his life cycle begins. Leaving holes in the pages for the reader's exploration, Eric Carle shows the caterpillar sampling a different kind and quantity of food each day. After eating his way through a variety of colorful foods and getting a stomach ache, the caterpillar consumes a green leaf, forms a cocoon, and undergoes the transformation into a brilliantly colored butterfly.

Before Reading the Book

- Find out what your students know about caterpillars. Make a chart that shows what we know and what we want to find out.
- Research to find out several different types of caterpillars and what they eat.
- Spring is a good time of year to bring caterpillars into the classroom to observe life cycle stages. Students can keep a "Care Chart" of the class caterpillars. (page 33) Check the Answer Key (page 112) for more details about classroom caterpillars.
- Students can make a booklet with drawings made at three or four day intervals to record their observations of the changes in the caterpillar.

While Reading the Book

- Look carefully at Eric Carle's illustrations and do some exploration with colored tissue paper collage technique. See page 8 for specific details.
- Sing the song "My Little Caterpillar" on page 34.
- Use sentence strips of the lyrics to "My Little Caterpillar." (page 35)
- Make picture cards (pages 36 and 37) and a tiny caterpillar (page 35 or a fuzzy pipe cleaner) to use with the song.

Students can draw outlines of foods for the caterpillar or you may enlarge the picture cards on pages 36 and 37. Use heavy paper, and have the children paint, color with marker or crayon, or fill in outlines using tissue paper collage. Cut or punch holes in the picture cards to show caterpillar bites. Children may use the picture cards to change the order of the foods that their caterpillar eats in the song. Picture cards can also be matched with word cards, or used to visualize addition and subtraction concepts.

After Reading the Book

- Make a caterpillar using thinned liquid laundry starch or thinned white glue to overlap several three inch circles (precut, free cut, or from the pattern on page 38) in shades of green tissue paper for the body and one red circle for the head on a 12" by 18" (30 cm x 46 cm) piece of white or light colored construction paper. Add details when dry with paint or marker.
- Make a "fold and paint butterfly." (page 39)
- Cut out several of the students' caterpillars and a butterfly to use on pages of a class Big Book to retell the story. Have small groups make collage fruits, leaves, and other foods for the book.

Caterpillar Care Chart

Teacher: You may use this chart as it is, or cover the words before duplication and create your own chart ideas to be copied within the caterpillar frame.

Caterpillar Care

1. Find a large, clear plastic jar or container with a lid. Ask a parent to help you poke air holes in the lid. (Silkworms can be kept in an open-topped box.)

2. Create a habitat for your caterpillar. It will need some dirt, sand, or pebbles on the bottom, and a stick to crawl up on when it is ready to form a cocoon. (Sticks are not necessary for silkworms.)

3. Place fresh leaves that your caterpillar likes in the habitat. (Mulberry leaves are good choices for silkworms.)

4. Gently put caterpillars in their habitat. Be sure habitat is located away from any heat source and not in direct sunlight.

5. Watch your caterpillars grow and change. Use a graph to record your observations.

6. Wait patiently. Do not bump or drop the habitat. Do not handle cocoons or touch them roughly.

7. After the butterflies or moths emerge, release them where you found the caterpillars.

"My Little Caterpillar"

The Caterpillar Song

Barbara Pelham 1992

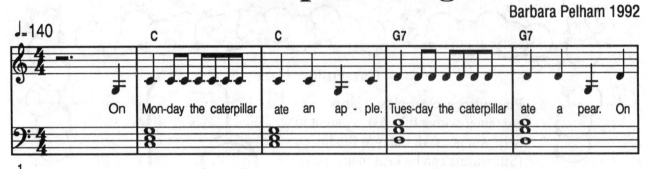

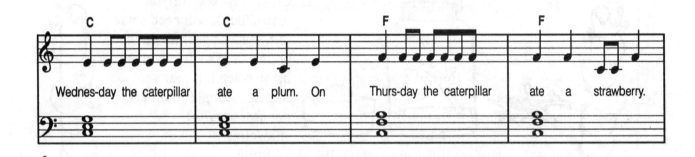

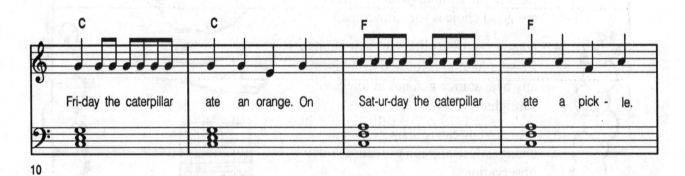

Teacher:

These lyrics can be reproduced as sentence strips for mini pocket charts. Picture cards can be used in place of food words (page 36 and 37) and the order of foods is interchangeable. Number words can be used instead of "a." ("On Tuesday the caterpillar ate two pears.") The little caterpillar at the right can be used as children sing the song.

"My Little Caterpillar"

On Monday the caterpillar ate an apple.

Tuesday the caterpillar ate a pear.

On Wednesday the caterpillar ate a plum.

On Thursday the caterpillar ate a strawberry.

Friday the caterpillar ate an orange.

On Saturday the caterpillar ate a pickle.

Sunday the caterpillar ate a leaf.

He isn't hungry anymore.

Picture Cards

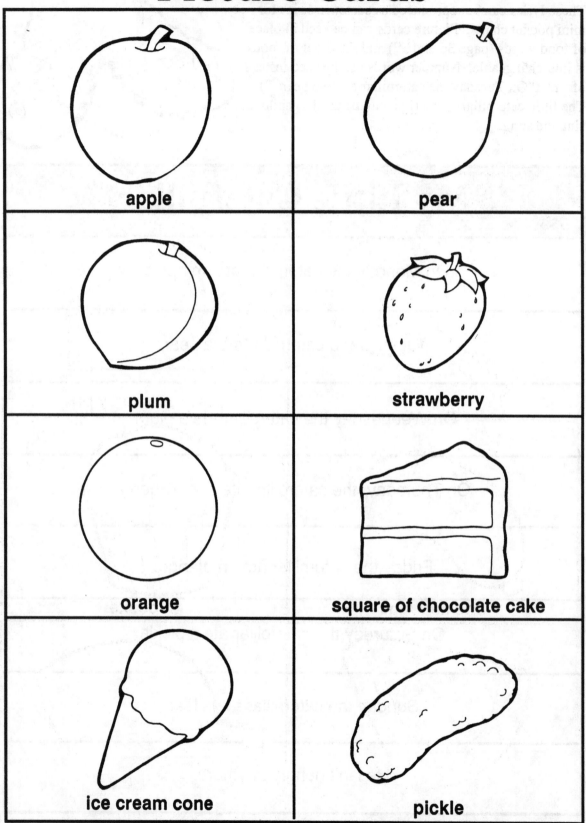

apple

pear

plum

strawberry

orange

square of chocolate cake

ice cream cone

pickle

Picture Cards

Swiss cheese

slice of salami

lollipop

piece of cherry pie

one sausage

cupcake

slice of watermelon

nice green leaf

Tissue Paper Collage
Caterpillar

Before starting this project, read the general instructions for tissue paper collage technique on page 8.

You will need:

* a 12" x 18" (30 cm x 45 cm) white piece of construction paper
* several 4 inch (10 cm) circles of green tissue (These can be free cut by students or traced from a pattern such as the one on this page.)
* one 4 inch (10 cm) circle of red for the head
* thinned white glue or liquid laundry starch
* paint brushes

1.

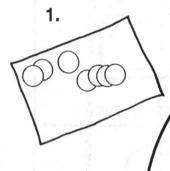

2.

Directions:

1. Place green circles overlapped on the white paper for the caterpillar's body. Brush on with starch or glue.

2. Add the head at one end and brush with starch or glue. Be sure all edges have been moistened.

3. When dry, add details with paint, crayon, marker, tissue or construction paper scraps, or fabric.

4. If desired, add a background of grass to white paper or cut around caterpillars and place them on class mural or in a class Big Book.

3.

4.

Fold and Paint Butterfly

Use the pattern on this page to cut a butterfly wing shape from a folded piece of paper.

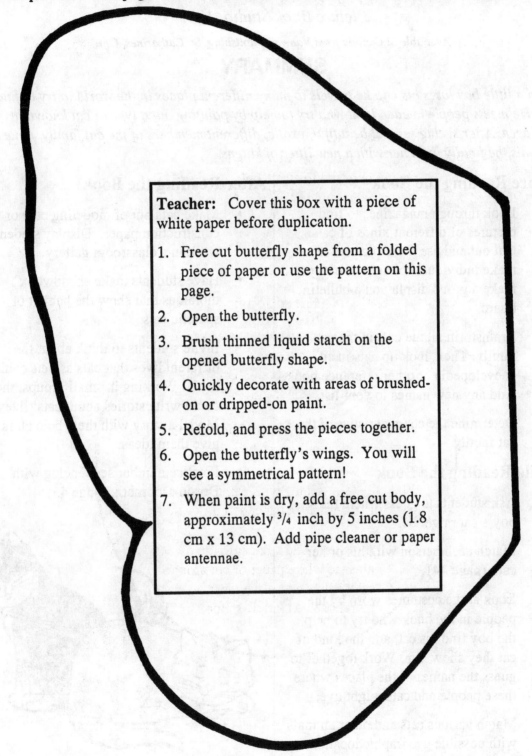

Teacher: Cover this box with a piece of white paper before duplication.

1. Free cut butterfly shape from a folded piece of paper or use the pattern on this page.

2. Open the butterfly.

3. Brush thinned liquid starch on the opened butterfly shape.

4. Quickly decorate with areas of brushed-on or dripped-on paint.

5. Refold, and press the pieces together.

6. Open the butterfly's wings. You will see a symmetrical pattern!

7. When paint is dry, add a free cut body, approximately ³/₄ inch by 5 inches (1.8 cm x 13 cm). Add pipe cleaner or paper antennae.

These butterflies make a beautiful display hung from the ceiling or on a bulletin board.

Have You Seen My Cat?

by Eric Carle

Picture Book Studio, 1987

Available in Canada from Vanwell Publishing, St. Catharines, Ont.

SUMMARY

When a little boy loses his cat, he travels to many different places in the world to try to find her. He meets people in each land who try to help by pointing out a type of cat known in their area. After seeing several beautiful, exotic, different members of the cat family, none of them his, he finally finds her with a new litter of kittens.

Before Reading the Book

- Look through magazines to find pictures of different kinds of cats. Cut out and use these pictures to make individual collages of cats or make a group display on a bulletin board.

- Brainstorm all the cats in the cat family. Then, look up cats in an encyclopedia or other reference book. Add any new names to your list.

- Determine the characteristics of the cat family.

While Reading the Book

- Ask students to guess where the boy's cat might be.

- Match each person with his or her cat. (page 44)

- Look at the costumes worn by the people in the book who try to help the boy find his cat, and the kind of cat they show him. Work together to guess the names of the places where these people and cats might live.

- Match various cats and other animals with possible geographic locations. (page 41-43)

After Reading the Book

- Make cats out of modeling clay or construction paper. Display students' work in a classroom gallery.

- Have students make shadowbox dioramas that show the habitat of specific cats.

- Invite students to think about the different lives that cats as pets could have. Working in small groups, they could write stories about cats' lives. Model a story with the whole class to give them ideas.

- Practice number sequencing with Dot-to-Dot math. (page 45)

Where Is My Home?

Using encyclopedias and other resources and the world map on pages 43-44, cut out and glue the picture of each member of the cat family near the continent where it lives.

Lion

Bobcat

Cheetah

Puma *(Mountain Lion)*

Tiger

Jaguar

World Map

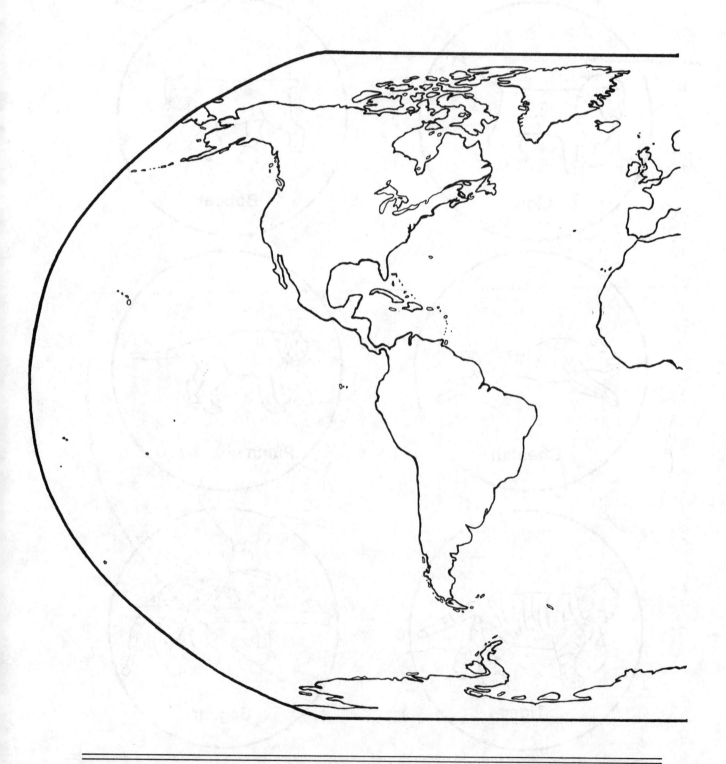

World Map (cont.)

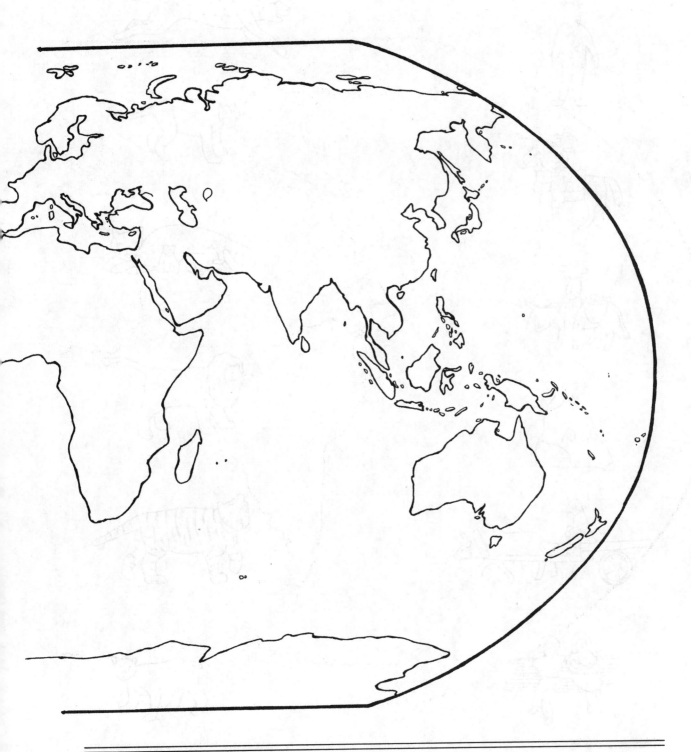

Cat Match!

Draw a line from each person in the story to the cat found where he or she lives. Use the book to help you!

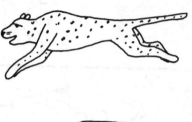

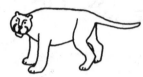

Name

Directions: Connect the dots from 1 to 50. Then color me.

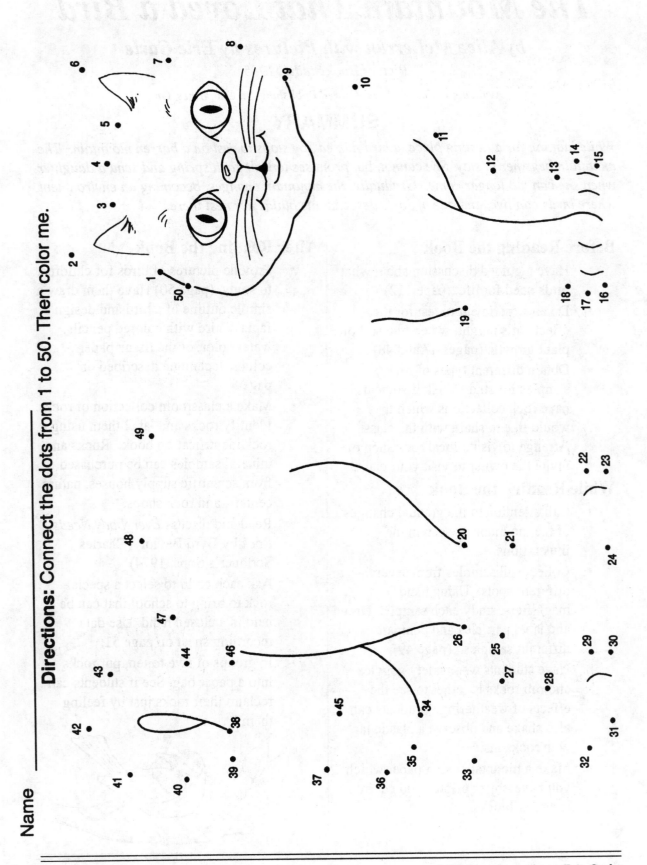

The Mountain That Loved a Bird

by Alice McLerran with Pictures by Eric Carle

Picture Book Studio, 1985

Available in Canada from Vanwell Publishing, St. Catharines, Ont.

SUMMARY

While hunting for a nesting place, a bird named Joy stops to rest on a barren mountain. The mountain begs her to stay. She cannot, but promises to visit each spring and send a daughter when she can no longer come. Gradually, the mountain changes, becoming an environment where birds can live, and one of Joy's descendants builds her nest there.

Before Reading the Book

- Have a guided discussion about what birds need for life. (page 112)
- Do an experiment to test for the effects of sunlight, water, and soil on plant growth. (pages 47 and 48)
- Obtain different types of rock samples for study. Ask if students have rock collections which they would like to share with the class. Arrange to visit a local rock shop or invite the owner to visit your class.

While Reading the Book

- Call attention to the gradual changes of the mountain as seen in the illustrations.
- Collect soil samples from several different spots. Using hand magnifiers, study each sample. Draw and label particles and compare different samples. (page 49)
- Have students wear safety goggles and rub rocks together to see the effects of weathering. Students can also shake and observe a plastic jar with rocks inside.
- Make a mountain using paper which you have object printed and cut into irregular blocks.

After Reading the Book

- Provide pictures of birds for children to study. (page 50) Have them draw a simple outline of a bird and design a fantasy bird with colored pencils, water color, or the tissue paper collage technique described on page 8.
- Make a classroom collection of rocks. Identify rocks and label them using a rock identification book. Rocks and mineral samples can be purchased from scientific supply houses, nature centers, and rock shops.
- Read and discuss *Everybody Needs A Rock* by Byrd Baylor. (Charles Scribner's Sons, 1974)
- Ask each child to select a special rock to bring to school that can be held in a closed hand. Use data recording sheet on page 51.
- In groups of five to ten, put rocks into a paper bag. See if students can reclaim their rocks just by feeling them.

This project can be done as a whole class activity or in small groups of two to six.

What Do Plants Need?

QUESTION: Under what conditions will seeds grow best?

HYPOTHESIS: We think that the seeds planted in cup #_____ will grow best because plants need _____

Cup #	What Is Missing?	What Will Happen To These Seeds?
1		
2		
3		
4		
5		

PROCEDURE:

Materials Needed:

5 clear plastic cups
tape and pen for label
radish or grass seed
small rocks or pebbles
garden soil
water

Steps:

1. Label the containers #1 to #5.

2. Fill container #1 half-full of rocks, a half-cup of garden soil, 5 seeds, and 2 tablespoons (25 mL) of water. Keep in a sunny spot.

3. Fill container #2 half-full of rocks, a half-cup of garden soil, 5 seeds, and 2 tablespoons of water. Keep in a dark spot.

4. Fill container #3 half-full of rocks, a half-cup of garden soil, 5 seeds, do not water, and keep in a sunny spot.

5. Fill container #4 half-full of rocks, 5 seeds, 2 tablespoons of water, and keep in a sunny spot.

6. Fill container #5 with a half-cup of garden soil, 5 seeds, 2 tablespoons of water, and keep in a sunny spot.

Record the RESULTS and CONCLUSIONS on the observation sheet on page 48.

Observation Sheet

In a three week period, observe the degree of seed growth on this chart. Draw and date your observations.

Week 1					
	#1	#2	#3	#4	#5
Week 2					
	#1	#2	#3	#4	#5
Week 3					
	#1	#2	#3	#4	#5

Conclusions:

Our hypothesis was/was not supported. Seeds grow best in container # _____ because

_____

_____

A Closer Look!

Collect soil samples from several different spots. Using hand magnifiers, study each sample. Draw what you see in these magnifiers.

My Fantasy Bird

The mountain waited year after year for Joy to return. The bird made a difference in the mountain's life, bringing color, music, and hope to a place that had previously been barren of these things.

Suppose you were to create a bird that could inspire others, such as Joy had done for the mountain. What would your fantasy bird look like?

Here are several different types of birds. Practice drawing bird details such as beaks, wings, feet, tail feathers, and eyes. Then, draw an outline of a bird on a piece of art paper. Use colored pencils, water color, or the tissue paper collage technique described on page 8 to fill in the outline with your "fantasy" bird! When you have finished, you may want to write or tell a story about what makes your bird so special!

My Rock!

My rock's name:

_____

Draw a picture of your rock. Be sure to put in as many details as possible

Size:

measured top to bottom: _____

measured front to back: _____

measured side to side: _____

Color: _____

Texture: _____

Weight: _____

Surface: _____

Hardness: _____

Buoyancy: _____

What kind of a rock do you think it is? Why?

_____

_____

_____

The Tiny Seed

by Eric Carle
(Picture Book Studio, 1987)

Available in Canada from Vanwell Publishing, St. Catharines, Ont.

SUMMARY

A tiny seed manages to grow and thrive despite many odds against its survival. Eric Carle has written and illustrated a charming and inspirational story about the life cycle of a very special flower.

Before Reading the Book

- Ask students to explain what they know about:
  — the parts of a plant
  — what each plant part does
  — what a plant needs to live
  — the life cycle of a plant

- Invite your students to draw flowers of all kinds. Display the flowers on a "garden-like" bulletin board.

While Reading the Book

- Stage seed races. Include a wide variety of seeds as your contestants, such as dandelion, sunflower, marigold, acorn, watermelon, and other available types. Determine which seeds will travel the farthest with a gust of your breath. Record your predictions. Test each seed and measure the distance it traveled. Record your findings, and compare your predictions with the data you collected. Discuss the variety of ways seeds travel to insure their growth. (page 53)
- Learn about the parts (pages 54 and 55), needs, (pages 56 and 57) and life cycle (page 58) of a plant.
- Discuss seasons and plant growth.

After Reading the Book

- Try growing seeds in each of the environments mentioned in *The Tiny Seed*. (ice, water, sand, soil) Determine where a seed must be planted to survive. Review the Scientific Method. (page 59)
- Challenge students to rewrite the story from the point of view of the seed.
- Stage a plant growth cycle drama based on ideas from *The Tiny Seed*. Assign children to play the parts of the flying seeds, sun, mountains, ocean, desert, bird, mouse, big weed, child who steps on the flower, boy, girl, giant flower, birds, bees, butterflies, seedpods, and seeds. Present your drama for others.

Blow the Distance!

Record the results of your seed races on this chart.

Type of Seed	Illustration of Seed	Distance of Travel	Best Probable Method of Travel
1.			
2.			
3.			
4.			
5.			

Build a Plant!

Most plants have **ROOTS**, **STEMS**, **LEAVES**, **FLOWERS**, and **SEEDS**. Each part has a job to do in helping a plant live and grow.

ROOTS find and take in the water and minerals that a plant needs to live and grow. They also hold the plant in place.

STEMS carry water and minerals from the roots to the leaves. They also carry the food made in the leaves to all parts of the plant. Stems are the main roadways in plants. Also, stems hold the leaves and flowers up in the air so they can get sunlight.

LEAVES make food for a plant to live and grow. Leaves are filled with chlorophyll. Cholorophyll's job is to catch the sunlight to help the leaves make food for the plant. It is chlorophyll that gives a leaf its green color.

FLOWERS hold the parts of the plant that helps it reproduce, which means to make more plants. When flowers bloom, it is a sign that plants are ready to make seeds.

SEEDS have the job of making new plants. Sometimes seeds can be found inside the flower of a plant, like sunflower seeds. Sometimes seeds can be found on the ground, like an acorn. Sometimes seeds can be found flying in the wind, like the seeds of a dandelion!

Directions: Cut apart the boxes and glue them on a piece of construction paper in the order they would occur in nature. Then draw your own plants with all their parts. Be sure you can name each part and decribe something that it does.

The Parts of a Plant

Draw a line from each word to the
part of the plant it names. Then, on
the lines tell what that part does.

seed

_____

_____

_____

leaf

_____

_____

_____

root

_____

_____

_____

flower

_____

_____

_____

stem

_____

_____

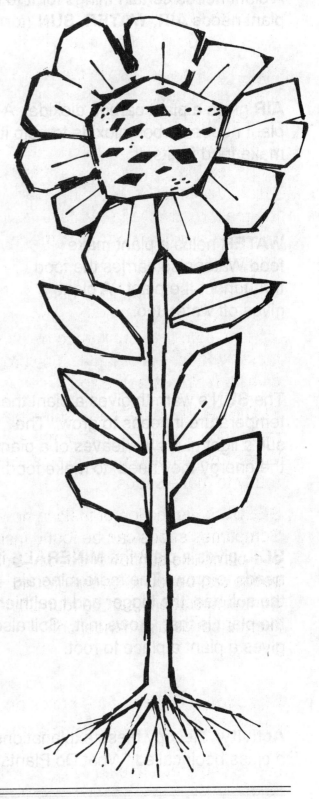

Give Me These, Please!

A plant needs certain things for it to live and grow, just like you do. A plant needs **AIR**, **WATER**, **SUN** (for warmth and light), and **MINERALS**.

AIR gives a plant carbon dioxide. A plant needs carbon dioxide to help it make food for itself.

WATER helps a plant make food. Water also carries the food throughout the plant. A plant gives off water, too.

The **SUN**'s warmth gives a plant the temperature it needs to grow. The sun's light gives the leaves of a plant the energy they need to make food.

SOIL gives a plant the **MINERALS** it needs to grow. The more minerals the soil has, the bigger and healthier the plant is that grows in it. Soil also gives a plant a place to root.

Activity: Recopy these explanations and illustrate each concept to make a class book called "What Do Plants Need To Live?"

Which Is Best for Plant Growth?

Have you ever wondered what plants can grow in best? Can they grow best in sand, or dirt, or potting soil, or water? If this makes you curious, try this scientific investigation.

Question:
Does a plant grow better in sand or dirt?

Hypothesis:
A plant grows better in _____ .

Procedure:

Materials: two clear plastic cups; four sunflower seeds; sand; dirt

Step-By-Step Directions:

1. Fill one cup with sand and the other with dirt.
2. Label each cup "sand" or "dirt."
3. Plant two sunflower seeds in each cup.
4. Put both cups next to each other in a sunny window.
5. Water them every day for two weeks.

Results:
Draw a picture of what happened to the plants.

Conclusions:
The results show that my hypothesis was/was not supported.

A sunflower plant grows better in _____ than _____.

What do you wonder next?

_____

_____

_____

_____

Sequence of a Life Cycle

Color and cut out these cards. Arrange them in life cycle order.

The Scientific Method

The study of plants provides an excellent opportunity for your students to learn or review the scientific method.

Review of the Scientific Method

Scientists ask questions and try to find the answers in a way that is known as the scientific method.

These are the steps that they follow:

1. **QUESTION:** A scientist asks a question about something that makes him or her wonder.

   Example: Can you grow a healthy plant in darkness?

2. **HYPOTHESIS**: A scientist makes a guess as to the answer to the question.

   Example: I cannot grow a healthy plant in darkness.

3. **PROCEDURE:** A scientist develops a plan to support or not support the hypothesis.

   Example: I will test my hypothesis by trying to grow two plants that are the same size, one in darkness and one in light. I will water them with exactly the same amounts of water.

4. **RESULTS:** A scientist measures and records what happens in the investigation.

   Example: I will record the growth of each plant in centimeters every other day on a graph. I will also check the plant's color and leaf growth.

5. **CONCLUSIONS:** A scientist evaluates what he or she has discovered from the results.

   Example: My hypothesis was supported. The plant that had light grew healthily, and the plant that had no light did not grow healthily.

Ask your students what plants make them wonder.

Examples:

Do roots change direction to find water?

Can a plant grow without leaves?

If a plant's stem is cut half-way through, will the plant survive?

Will a plant turn toward light?

These and other questions about plants can be investigated easily by a primary student. Encourage your students to plan for these investigations in a scientific manner.

The Grouchy Ladybug

by Eric Carle

Crowell, 1986

Available in Canada from Harper Collins, Canada

SUMMARY

Angrily leaving a leaf full of aphids that it did not want to share with another ladybug, the grouchy ladybug flew off in search of a fight. Each hour of the day it encountered an opponent that it felt was just "not big enough" to fight. By the end of the day, the grouchy ladybug was ready to challenge a whale. But the whale, with a slap of his tail, sent the ladybug back toward land. Wet, hungry, and tired, the grouchy ladybug once again was offered the chance to share aphids with the friendly ladybug. This time, the offer was graciously accepted!

Before Reading the Book

- Discuss the importance of sharing.
- Introduce or review the concepts of seconds, minutes, and hours. Play time-estimating, games related to seconds, minutes, and hours to make time concepts real. (page 61)
- Instruct students in time-telling skills. Include a discussion of the second hand, the minute hand, and the hour hand. (page 62)
- Practice telling time. Use the blank form on page 63 by either filling in the times to be told by drawing on the clocks, or the times to be drawn by writing the time on the blank lines.

While Reading the Book

- Make "Ladybug Clocks." (pages 64 and 65) Encourage students to pair up for telling time practice, each partner using his or her own clock to "quiz" the other partner in time-telling skills.
- Discuss aggressive behavior and its consequences.

- Present size-comparison concepts, such as bigger than, smaller than, and equal to, as they relate to the ladybug and other creatures in the story.
- Reread the story of the grouchy ladybug in class, while students use their "Ladybug Clocks" to make each time as you read the story. Ask them to take their clocks home to help them tell the story to their families.

After Reading the Book

- Dramatize the story with the children playing the parts of all the animals.
- Research the ladybug's role as a garden helper.
- Create a story of the grouchy ladybug's next day.

Seconds, Minutes, or Hours?

Can these things be best measured in seconds, minutes, or hours? Write your answer on the blank for each question. When you have finished, compare your time ideas with others in class or at home.

1. How long does it take to walk to a friend's house?

_____

2. How long does it take to give a hug?

_____

3. How long does it take to sneeze?

_____

4. How long does it take to eat lunch?

_____

5. How long does it take you to fall asleep once you are in bed for the night?

_____

6. How long does it take you to watch the colors in a sunset change?

_____

7. How long does it take you to eat an ice cream cone?

_____

8. How long does it take to clean your room? _____

9. How long does it take to count to 100? _____

10. How long does it take to watch a movie? _____

11. How long does it take to brush your teeth? _____

12. How long does it take to read a story? _____

13. How long does it take to get to a vacation spot? _____

14. How long can you ride a bike? _____

15. How long does it take to walk a dog? _____

Think of more "How long does it take?" ideas of your own!

Time Telling

Learning to tell time is fun. It is like a game. You have to be able to read numbers on a clock's "face" by the positions of the clock's "hands."

This is a "face" of a clock. The face has the numbers 1 to 12 written on it.

These are the "hands" of a clock. The hand that measures minutes is longer than the hand that measures hours.

Each hour is marked on the clock in a special way. The minute hand points to the twelve, and the hour hand points to the hour it is.

Half hours are marked on the clock with the minute hand pointing to the six, and the hour hand halfway between two numbers.

Quarter hours are marked on the clock with the minute hand pointing either to the three or the nine. The hour hand is either one-fourth or three-fourths past the hour number.

Knowing how to tell time is very important. Practice daily!

Telling Time Practice

Show that you understand how to tell time by completing the times below.

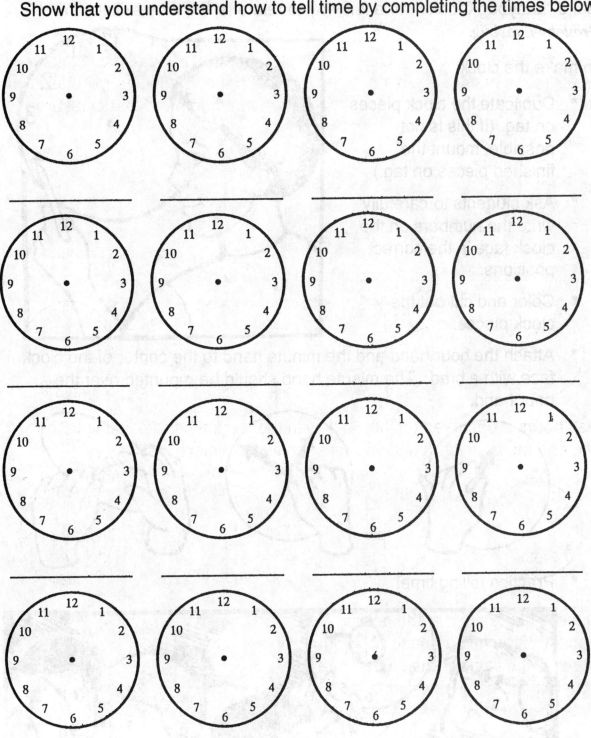

Teacher: Program this sheet to match the skills you are teaching.

Ladybug Clocks

Make "Ladybug Clocks" for a fun way to relate telling time skills to *The Grouchy Ladybug*.

To make the clock:

*   Duplicate the clock pieces on tag. (If this is not possible, mount the finished pieces on tag.)

*   Ask students to carefully write the numbers on the clock face in the correct positions.

*   Color and cut out the clock pieces.

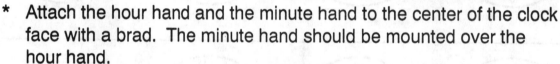

*   Attach the hour hand and the minute hand to the center of the clock face with a brad. The minute hand should be mounted over the hour hand.

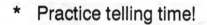
*   Practice telling time!

Ladybug Clocks

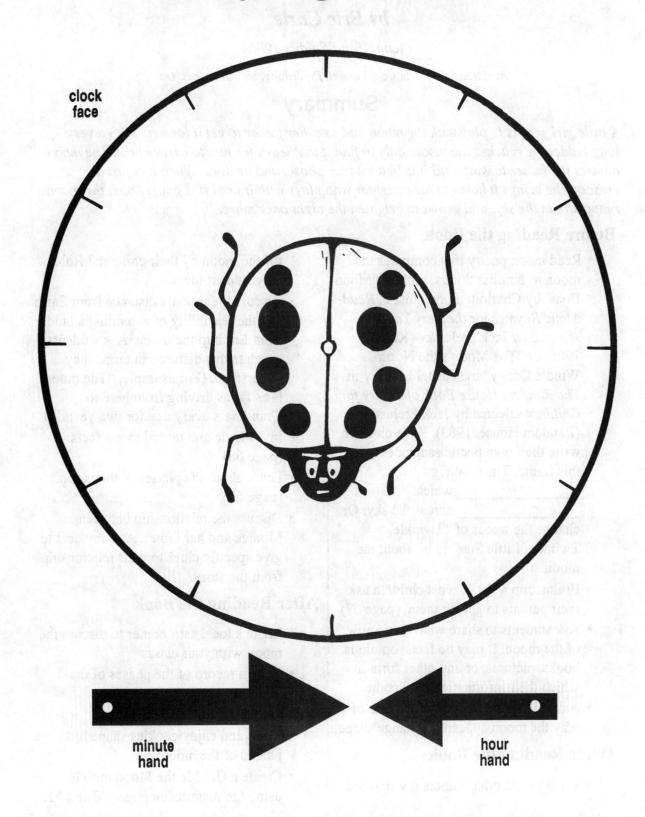

clock
face

minute
hand

hour
hand

Papa, Please Get the Moon for Me

by Eric Carle

Picture Book Studio, 1986

Available in Canada from Vanwell Publishing, St. Catharines, Ont.

Summary

A little girl yearns to play with the moon and asks her father to get it for her. With a very long ladder, he reaches the moon, only to find it too heavy for him to carry home. The moon advises the father to wait until it is in a smaller phase, and he does. When it is just a crescent, he brings it home to his daughter who plays with it until it is gone. Soon, the moon reappears in the sky, and grows to brighten the night once more.

Before Reading the Book

- Read moon poetry that compares the moon to familiar things, such as "Moon Boat" by Charlotte Pomerantz in *Read-Aloud Rhymes for the Very Young* selected by Jack Prelutsky (Knopf, 1986) or "The Moon's the North Wind's Cooky" by Vachel Lindsay in *The Random House Book of Poetry for Children* selected by Jack Prelutsky (Random House, 1983). Have children write their own poetic sentences using this frame: The moon is a _____ which _____ across the sky. Or, change the words of "Twinkle, Twinkle, Little Star" to be about the moon.
- Brainstorm a list of what children ask their parents to get for them. (page 67)
- Ask students to share what they know of the moon. It may be facts, opinions, books, pictures, or any other form in which their information may come.
- Ask children to explain their ideas of why the moon appears to change shape.

While Reading the Book

- What would other fathers say if asked for the moon by their children? Role play student ideas.
- Discuss the moon's distance from Earth and the feasibility of extending a ladder from Earth to the moon. Ask students to relate this distance in terms they understand. (For example, "The moon is as far as driving from here to Grandma's every day for two years!")
- Investigate and record moon facts. (page 68)
- Learn about the phases of the moon. (page 69)
- Discuss the relationship between Monica and her father. Ask students to give specific clues to their relationship from the story.

After Reading the Book

- Invite a local astronomer to discuss the moon with your class.
- Keep a record of the phases of the moon on a monthly calendar.
- Go for a moonlit hike.
- Make and enjoy cookies shaped like the phases of the moon!
- Create a Get Me the Moon mobile using the patterns on pages 70 and 71.

Please, May I Have It!

On the ladder make a list of the things you might be likely to ask your parents to get for you.

How many of the things on your list might be things your parents could actually get you? Write the word "yes" next to these things.

How many of the things on your list would you have absolutely no chance of ever getting from your parents? Write the word "never" next to these things.

How many of the things on your list is there a possibility that your parents might get for you? Write the word "maybe" next to these things.

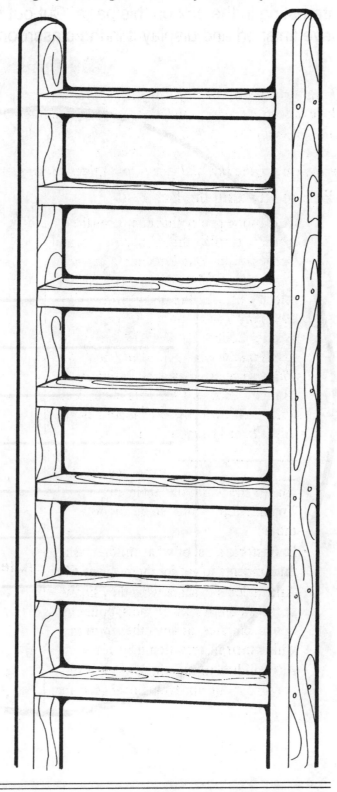

Moon Facts

Research to discover facts about the moon. Write a fact you find interesting in the box on this page. Cut out the moon shape when you have finished and display it in the classroom.

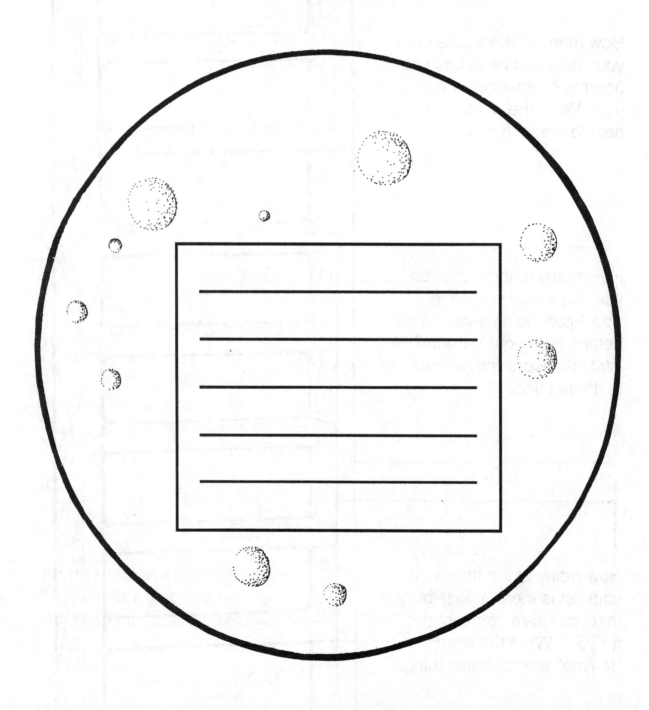

We See the Moon

The moon is the closest and brightest object we can see from Earth at night, but the moon does not make its own light. The moon reflects the light of the sun, and what we see as moonlight, is really reflected sunlight. If you watch the sky for a month, it seems as if the moon changes in size and shape. This is because we can only see the sunlit part of the moon that is facing Earth.

Draw each moon in the boxes.

Full Moon

During a **full moon** we can see all of the moon's sunlit surface.

Half Moon

During a **half moon** we see only half of the moon's sunlit surface.

Crescent Moon

During a **crescent moon** we see only a sliver of the moon's sunlit surface.

Get Me the Moon Mobile

Color and cut out the moon, star, girl and Papa (pages 70-71). Punch holes and tie yarn through each. Attach varied lengths of yarn at different places on a coat hanger. Display mobiles around the room. (See diagram below.)

Get Me the Moon Mobile *(cont.)*

The Mixed-Up Chameleon

by Eric Carle
Harper Collins, 1984

Available in Canada from Harper Collins, Canada

SUMMARY

A chameleon, able to change color to blend with its environment or with temperature changes, becomes discontent with its life. Upon a visit to a zoo, the chameleon wishes to become quite a variety of animals. In Eric Carle's clever artwork, we see the combination of animals the chameleon believes to be perfect. However, it soon realizes that it is no longer equiped to catch a fly for its meal. The mixed-up chameleon quickly wishes to be itself again, and happily catches the fly.

Before Reading the Book

- Make composite people and/or animal pages. (page 73)
- Discuss animals your students would like to be and why.
- Ask your students if they have ever wanted to be someone else. Encourage explanations.
- Invite students to participate in "All About Me" activities. (pages 74 and 75)

While Reading the Book

- Study the chameleon and its ability to change color. If possible, bring a chameleon in for class study.
- After each change the chameleon makes, ask students how they think the new part can help or hinder the chameleon.
- As you read the story, ask the students to make their own "cumulative" drawing.
- Create your own "I wish I could _____ like a _____" books.

After Reading the Book

- Write a class story about what the mixed up chameleon's life might have been like had it not wished itself back to normal.
- Make "Mixed-Up People" books. (pages 76 and 77)
- Over a period of a week, not all on one day, play "What makes you special." Ask your students to sit in a circle. Choose one student to sit in the center of the circle. Several class members then take turns telling that person something that is special (and complimentary) about him or her.

Look at This!

Have you ever tried to put the heads, arms, or legs of different people on each other?

Look through consumable magazines and cut out pictures you think might be good to make a composite picture such as the one on the right. Carefully cut out body parts and glue them on tagboard or construction paper.

Make a display of your composite people!

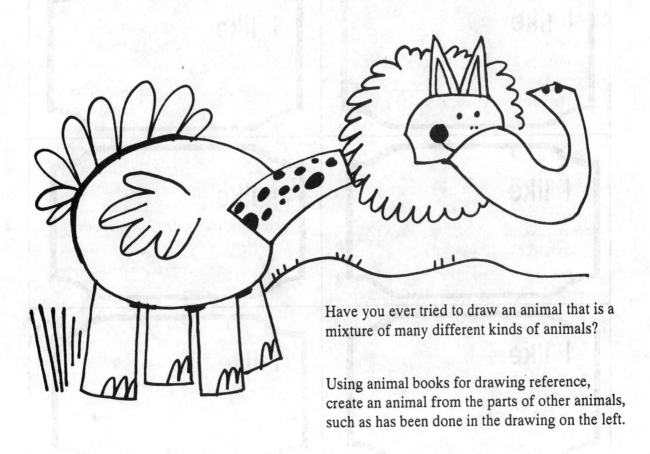

Have you ever tried to draw an animal that is a mixture of many different kinds of animals?

Using animal books for drawing reference, create an animal from the parts of other animals, such as has been done in the drawing on the left.

Make a display of your new animals!

All About Me

The mixed-up chameleon did not feel good about being a chameleon because it did not like who it was and wished to be something else.

Do you feel good about who you are? Learning about ourselves takes a long time. Sometimes we know right away what things make us special. Sometimes it takes years to discover those special things.

Many things about us are different from others, and many things are the same. Whatever our differences or similarities, it is good to remember that we all have one very powerful ability in common — we can like who we are!

Fill in these cards with things you like about yourself. You may like your hair color or style, your ability to play a certain sport, the way you help your friends and family, or how you read, spell, solve math problems, and smile! After you have filled out your cards, cut them apart and keep them where you can read them when you need a boost! Make as many cards as you want!

A Poem About Me

The mixed-up chameleon wanted to be many things it was not. But, being what it was not did not make it happy. It found out that being itself was best. Find out about yourself by completing the poem below.

I am _____

_____

and _____

But I am not _____

I like _____

_____

and _____

But I do not like _____

I am happy when _____

_____

and _____

But I am not happy when _____

I feel good about myself when _____

and _____

But I do not feel good about myself when _____

_____

If I could be anything, I would be _____

_____

and _____

But, even though I could be anything,

I would not be _____

Mixed-Up People!

The mixed-up chameleon was quite a combination of animals when it had completed its wishing!

Have you ever wished to be someone else? Perhaps you have wanted someone's hair or eye color, or athletic legs, or attractive clothes. Now's your chance to put the new you together!

For this project, you will need a copy of page 77 duplicated on tag or other heavy paper. Each member of your class will need this page.

1. Cut out the outside rectangle that has been duplicated on tag for you.

2. Draw your head from the neck up in the top section. If you have long hair, do not draw past the top box yet.

3. Draw your body to the waist and the clothes you like to wear in the middle section. If you have long hair, you may now add it in.

4. Draw your body from the waist down and the clothes you like to wear in the bottom section. Add your favorite shoes, too.

5. Carefully cut on the solid lines between the top and middle section, and the middle and bottom section. Do not cut beyond the dashed lines. Fold on the dotted lines.

6. Staple your page to the pages of five to ten of your classmates. Flip through the book and create a new you!

Mixed-Up People!

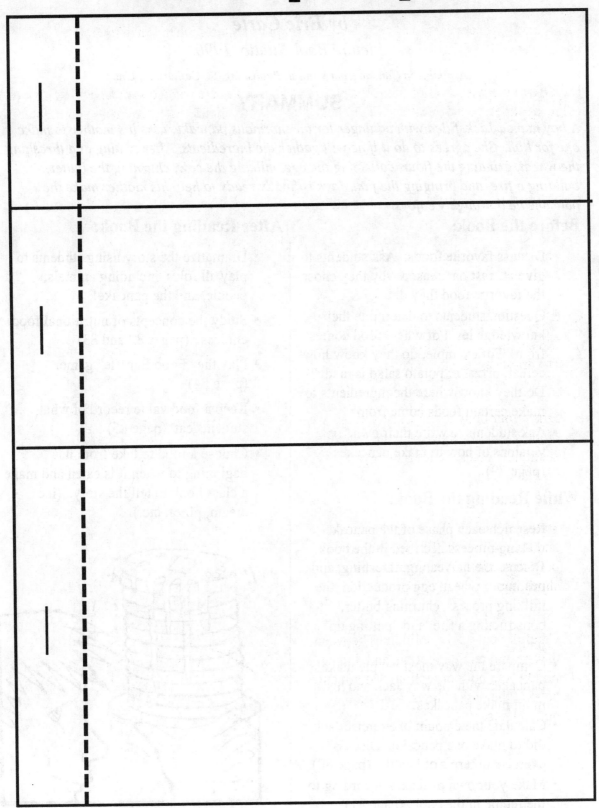

Pancakes, Pancakes!

by Eric Carle
Picture Book Studio, 1990

Available in Canada from Vanwell Publishing, St. Catharines, Ont.

SUMMARY

A boy named Jack, filled with a hunger for an enormous pancake, asks his mother to make one for him. She agrees to do it if he will gather the ingredients. After cutting and threshing the wheat, grinding the flour, collecting the egg, milking the cow, churning the butter, building a fire, and bringing the jam, Jack is finally ready to help his mother make the pancake he thoroughly enjoys!

Before the Book:

- Discuss favorite foods. Ask students to give at least one reason why they chose the favorite food they did.
- Question students to determine their knowledge level of where food comes from. For example, do they know how cereal, pizza, or potato salad is made? Do they know where the ingredients to make certain foods come from?
- Ask students to write their own versions of how to make pancakes. (page 79)

While Reading the Book:

- Research each phase of the pancake-making process decribed in the book. Discuss the harvesting, threshing, and milling of wheat, egg production, the milking process, churning butter, constructing a fire, and "putting up" jam.
- Compare the way most people make pancakes with the way Jack and his mom make pancakes.
- Calculate the amount of exercise Jack did to make one pancake. Discuss exercise in terms of health. (page 80)
- Make your own pancakes according to the recipe in the book. (page 81)

After Reading the Book:

- Dramatize the story using students to play all roles, including animals, people, and the pancake!
- Study the concepts of nutritional food choices. (pages 82 and 83)
- Play the "Food Shuffle" game. (page 84)
- Keep a food value record of what students eat. (page 85)
- Choose a food to take from its beginning to when it is eaten and make a class book to tell the story. (ice cream, pizza, etc.)

How Do You Make a Pancake?

On the recipe card below, give directions for making a pancake. Be sure to include all the steps you think are necessary.

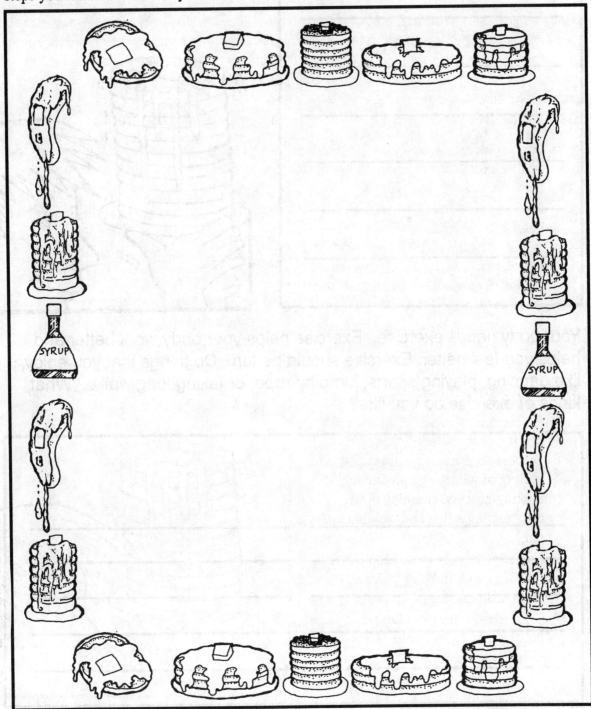

Exercise!

Jack did more than sit down at the table and eat a pancake. He had to work for his meal. Make a list of all the things Jack had to do for his pancake that could be counted as exercise for his body.

Your body needs exercise. Exercise helps your body work better and helps you feel better. Exercise should be fun. Do things that you enjoy, like dancing, playing sports, jumping rope, or taking long walks. What kinds of exercise do you like?

Mix, Cook, and Eat!

Jack and his mother made a pancake with just a few simple ingredients. It's your turn to try their recipe!

Supplies you will need:

- mixing bowl
- cup measure
- a wooden spoon
- a ladle
- a frying pan
- a spatula
- a plate
- a knife, fork, and spoon

Ingredients you will need:

- one cup (250 mL) of flour
- one egg
- one cup of milk
- a pat of butter
- strawberry jam

1. Measure a cup of flour and put it in the mixing bowl.

2. Break an egg over the mixing bowl and stir it into the flour. (No shells, please!)

3. Pour a cup of milk into the bowl and mix it with the flour and egg until the mixture is smooth without any lumps.

4. With adult supervision heat a frying pan. Melt a pat of butter in the pan.

5. Scoop a ladleful of batter out of the bowl and pour it slowly into the hot pan.

6. After the top of the pancake bubbles, turn it over with a spatula. Cook both sides until they are golden brown.

7. Use the spatula to lift the pancake to your plate. Spread with strawberry jam and enjoy!

Nutritional Food Choices

You need to eat! You need to eat so you can have energy to work and play. Eating helps your body grow and stay healthy.

Some foods help your body more than others. Choosing the right foods to eat is very important to your health. When you eat the right foods, your body can get the ingredients it needs for energy, growth, and staying healthy.

The food ingredients your body needs to stay alive and healthy are called nutrients. Your body needs these six nutrients:

Proteins help build and repair your body. As you grow and need bigger muscles and organs, proteins help to build them. When you scrape or cut yourself, proteins help to repair your skin. Some foods with protein are meat, milk, nuts, beans, and eggs.

Carbohydrates give your body fuel for energy. When you eat carbohydrates, you have enough energy to run, work, and play for a long time. There are two types of carbohydrates—starch and sugar. Some foods with starch are bread, cereal, and rice. Some foods with sugar are fruits, like oranges and apples.

Fats give your body fuel for energy. Fats do something else, too. The layer of fat under your skin helps keep your body warm. Some foods with fat are cheese and nuts.

Vitamins help you grow and help you use your food. Some vitamins even protect you from disease. Vitamins A and C help fight infections. Vitamins C and D help your bones to be strong and well-formed. Vitamin B helps your proteins, carbohydrates, and fats get used by your body. Some foods with vitamins are vegetables, whole grain breads and cereals, nuts, fruit, and eggs. Vitamin D even comes from sunlight!

Minerals help you grow and help you use your food. Minerals also make your blood healthy. Some important minerals are calcium, phosphorus, and iron. Calcium helps your bones and teeth. Phosphorus helps your food get used properly. Iron makes your blood healthy. Some foods with these minerals are milk, eggs, grains, and fish.

Water is not a food, but you can't live without it. Over half of your body is made of water! Water helps to carry the other nutrients around your body. It helps you digest food and carry waste away. Water also helps keep your body at the right temperature. Almost all foods have water, especially fruits and vegetables.

A Balanced Diet

You can get the nutrients your body needs by eating a balanced diet. You have a balanced diet when the food you eat in your meals has the right amount of the six nutrients. One way you can have a balanced diet is to choose your meals from the four food groups. The *four food groups* are milk, bread and cereal, meat, and fruit and vegetables. Study the diagram below to learn how to balance what you eat each day.

The Eating Right Pyramid

A Guide to Daily Food Choices

KEY

● Fat (naturally occurring and added)

▼ Sugars (added)

These symbols show that fat and added sugars come mostly from fats, oils, and sweets, but can be part of or added to foods from the food groups as well.

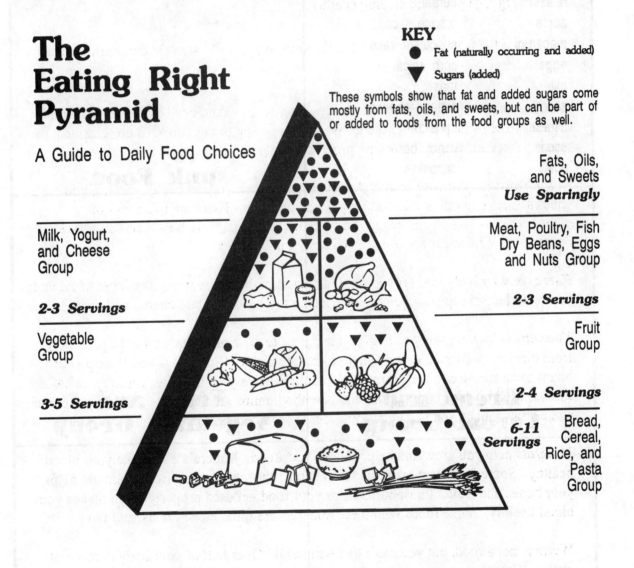

Milk, Yogurt, and Cheese Group

2-3 Servings

Vegetable Group

3-5 Servings

Fats, Oils, and Sweets
Use Sparingly

Meat, Poultry, Fish Dry Beans, Eggs and Nuts Group

2-3 Servings

Fruit Group

2-4 Servings

6-11 Servings Bread, Cereal, Rice, and Pasta Group

You must also remember to drink plenty of water. Your body really needs four to six 8 oz. (250 mL) glasses of water each day.

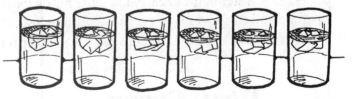

Food Shuffle!

These are the foods one very hungry child ate in one day. Look at each food. Rewrite the food in its food group box. If it is junk food, write the food in the junk food box.

beans	potato chips
carrots	tuna fish
raisins	cereal
apple	orange juice
macaroni	chocolate cake
eggs	corn chips
milk	toast
candy	cottage cheese
peanuts	tomato
soda	candy bar
rice	pancakes

Junk Food

Bread and Cereal Group

Fruit and Vegetable Group

Meat Group

Milk Group

Nutritional Planner

Plan a day's menu that includes the food choices needed to maintain good nutrition. Some foods you can use are in the box.

Bread and Cereal	Fruit and Vegetable	Meat	Milk
bread	carrots	beans	cottage cheese
cereal	apple	chicken	yogurt
rice	lettuce	beef	milk
macaroni	potatoes	eggs	cheese

Use this food group key in your planning chart:

Bread and Cereal Group = BC   *Meat Group* = Meat

Fruit and Vegetable Group = FV   *Milk Group* = Milk

Breakfast

_____ (group)

_____ (group)

_____ (group)

_____ (group

_____ (group)

Lunch

_____ (group)

_____ (group)

_____ (group)

_____ (group)

_____ (group)

Dinner

_____ (group)

_____ (group)

_____ (group)

_____ (group)

_____ (group

Snacks

_____ (group)

_____ (group)

1, 2, 3 to the Zoo

by Eric Carle

Philomel, 1968

Available in Canada from Putnam Publishing, Canada

SUMMARY

Following the engine of the train are full page illustrations of cars of zoo animals, each car containing one more than the last, from the first flat car with one elephant to the last boxcar filled with ten brightly colored birds. Each page has a diagram of the train at the bottom with the next car added. The last fold page shows the animals in their new homes at the zoo.

Before the Book

- Ask children if they have ever been to the zoo. If so, what kinds of animals did they see there? Write the names or draw pictures of some or all of the animals mentioned on the board or a chart.

- Discuss and reread some of your students' favorite counting books.

While Reading the Book

- Count the animals on each page of the book.

- Hunt for the mouse on each page.

- Do "Animal Math." (page 87)

- Discuss details in the illustrations. Ask questions such as "Can you find the blue snake?" or "What do you notice about these birds?"

- Match the numeral with the correct picture. (pages 88 and 89)

- Practice the movements of each animal you see.

After Reading the Book

- Play an "Animal Movement" game. Reproduce and cut out the numeral and animal cards from pages 88 and 89. (You may wish to enlarge them; reproduce them on heavy paper; and laminate them for durability.) Have a student choose an animal card and a numeral card. He or she then selects additional students so that there are performers equal to the number on the chosen card. These performers must then move like the chosen animal. Provide music or let students add sound effects. For example, if the bird and 9 card are chosen, nine students would act like birds. At the end of a given period of time or when the music stops, let another student choose new cards and begin again. Make sure all students have a chance to play.

- Engage in dramatic play. Ask small groups of children to pretend that they are in a train car on their way to the zoo. Ask them to show with their movements how the animals would look and move if they were tired, excited, happy, crowded, angry, nervous, or hungry. Have them show how they would feel in their new home.

- Play "1, 2, 3, to the Zoo Game." (pages 90 and 91)

Animal Math

Materials: numeral cards on page 88; beans; question cards below

Directions: Have children count the animals in *1,2,3 to the Zoo*. As the question is read, put the correct number of beans onto the numeral card.

1. Open the book and look at the first car on the train. How many elephants do you see? 	2. In the second car, how many hippos do you see? 
3. In the third car, how many giraffes do you see? 	4. Write and count beans for how many lions you see in the fourth car. 
5. In the fifth car, count the bears. 	6. How many alligators are in the sixth car? 
7. How many seals are in the seventh car? 	8. In the eighth car, how many monkeys can you find? 
9. Count the snakes in the ninth car. 	10. How many birds are in the tenth car? 

Numeral Cards

Cut out these cards on the heavy lines and match them with the correct animal card on page 89. These cards are also for use in the Animal Movement Game described on page 86 and Animal Math on page 87.

1	2
3	4
5	6
7	8
9	10

Animal Cards

Cut out these cards on the heavy lines and match them with the correct numeral card and/or animal name card on pages 88 and 91. These cards are also for use in the Animal Movement Game described on page 86.

1, 2, 3 to the Zoo Game

This game is full of physical activity and fun. Your students will beg to play it again and again!

- Duplicate six copies of the animal name cards from page 91 or the animal picture cards from page 89. Or, make a special card set by gluing the two sets back to back.

- Cut the cards out and stack them in like groups. You will only need five or six types of animals and their stacks for the first game.

- Ask children to sit in a large circle on chairs or carpet squares.

- Choose five or six stacks of cards and distribute them to your class to make five or six groups of five or six children. The other animal cards may be used in subsequent games.

- Take away one chair or carpet square and ask the standing child to call the name of one of the animals being used in the game. All the children with that animal name card must stand up and change seats. The first standing child tries to sit in one of their spots. The child who is left over then calls a different animal name.

- For some added fun, any caller may call out "1, 2, 3 to the Zoo!" instead of an animal name. Then all children must stand and find new places!

- You may choose to have children walk to their new places like the animal named on their cards.

- If this game is played in a small space, it would be a good idea to encourage walking!

Animal Name Cards

Use with game on page 90. These may also be used with the card sets on pages 88 and 89 for matching games.

elephant	**hippopotamus**
giraffe	**lion**
bear	**alligator**
seal	**monkey**
snake	**bird**

The Very Quiet Cricket

by Eric Carle
Philomel, 1990

Available in Canada from Putnam Publishing, Canada

SUMMARY

A tiny cricket hatches into a world filled with noise-making creatures who call out their welcomes to him. The baby cricket wants to answer, but cannot make a sound. By the end of the story, the cricket finds his voice, and we actually hear his sweet chirping as he discovers he can communicate in his world.

Before Reading the Book

- Find out how much your students know about crickets.

- Conduct the survey found on page 93.

- Ask students if they can easily make themselves understood by others. Encourage sharing.

- Make a tape recording of the voices of each of your students saying "Welcome!" "Good Morning," and "Hi!" (See directions on page 94.)

While Reading the Book

- Match the sounds with the animals that make them. (page 95)

- Predict if, how, and when the quiet cricket will find his voice.

- Study crickets. Label a diagram of a cricket. (page 96)

- Try to identify the taped-recorded voices of the students in the class. (page 94)

After Reading the Book

- Invite students to identify things about themselves that are unique. (page 97)

- Make tape recordings of various animals and their sounds. Ask others to try to identify the animal source of each recorded sound. Don't forget to make a key of the answers for your recording!

- Write a story about the noises the "quiet" cricket will make the next day!

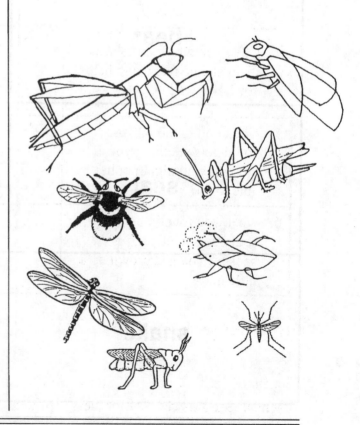

Has There Ever Been a Time?

Complete this survey verbally or in writing.

Has there ever been a time . . .?			
Questions	yes	no	Comments
1. when you were quiet even though you really wanted to say something?			
2. when many others could do something you could not do?			
3. when you tried to say something but could not be heard?			
4. when you didn't know what to do and no one could help you?			
5. when you found out you could do something you thought you might not be able to do?			
6. when you found out you could do something just because you had grown up a little more?			
7. when you helped other people understand that some things take time?			

Teacher: See Answer Key for ideas. (page 112)

Different Voices

Ask students to identify the tape-recorded voices of others in your class. To do this, just follow these instructions.

- Call students individually and privately to you over a period of one or two weeks. Assign each student a code number from 1 to the number of students in your class.

- On the tape, introduce a student by his or her number and give that student a short piece to read into the recorder. The selection should be at least fifteen seconds long and at an appropriate reading level. Do not let students know their numbers.

- Provide students with a list of the people that have been recorded. The list may be written on the board or reproduced for them on paper.

- Play the recording in class, asking students to place names of students by their numbered recordings. You may use the form on this page or one you devise.

#	Name	#	Name
1		17	
2		18	
3		19	
4		20	
5		21	
6		22	
7		23	
8		24	
9		25	
10		26	
11		27	
12		28	
13		29	
14		30	
15		31	
16		32	

Match These!

Draw a line from the words to the correct box.

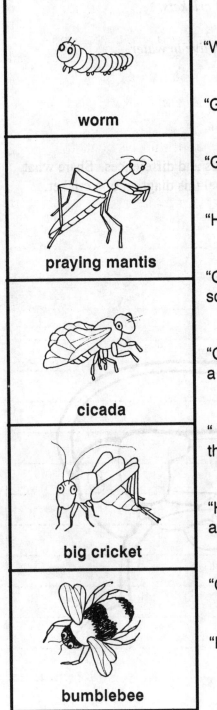

worm

praying mantis

cicada

big cricket

bumblebee

"Welcome!" chirped a

"Good day!" crunched a

"Good evening!" whirred a

"Hi!" bubbled a

"Good afternoon!" screeched a

"Good morning!" whizzed a

" . . . sailed quietly through the night

"How are you?" hummed a

"Good night!" buzzed the

"Hello!" whispered a

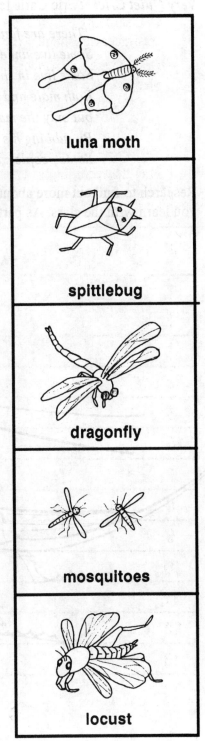

luna moth

spittlebug

dragonfly

mosquitoes

locust

About Crickets

All crickets are not the same, just as all people are not the same. At the beginning of *The Very Quiet Cricket* Eric Carle tells us more about these differences.

> *"There are four thousand different kinds of crickets.*
> *Some live underground, others above.*
> *Some live in shrubs or trees, and some even live in water.*
> *Both male and female crickets can hear,*
> *but only the male can make a sound.*
> *By rubbing his wings together he chirps.*
> *Some people say that it sounds like a song!"*

Research to find out more about crickets and their similarities and differences. Share what you learn with the class. As part of your research report, label this diagram of a cricket.

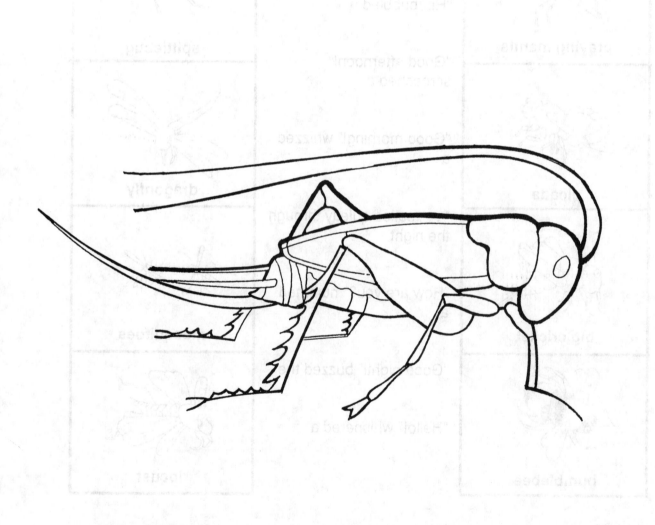

You Are Unique!

Trace one of your hands on this paper.

- On each of the fingers and the thumb, write something about you that is special. It could be the length or color of your hair, a hobby you enjoy, an activity you do well, something about you that others like, or a time you have felt proud of yourself.

- On the center of your palm, write a sentence that summarizes "who" you are. Here are some examples:

  "I am a friend to all animals."   *"I am a good rememberer."*

  "I am a good sister."   *"I am a great bike rider."*

- Cut out your finished hand and attach it to a class display.

The Mural

To celebrate all the vibrant illustrations in Eric Carle's books, as well as the playful spirit of his writing, invite your class to design and create an Eric Carle mural. Constructing this mural will demonstrate their skill and creativity with tissue paper collage technique, showcase their knowledge of the books you have studied, and provide them with hours of fun!

Art suggestions and patterns will be found on pages 100-103. Decide how you will group your students for work on the mural. Here are some ideas.

Characters and Background

Assign one-half of the class to Eric Carle characters with each student choosing a specific one. Assign the other half of the class

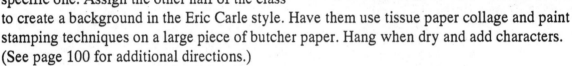

to create a background in the Eric Carle style. Have them use tissue paper collage and paint stamping techniques on a large piece of butcher paper. Hang when dry and add characters. (See page 100 for additional directions.)

Montage

This display is a montage of one book character overlayed upon another. Each student creates one character to add.

The Mural *(cont.)*

Sectioned Bulletin Board

This bulletin board is divided into separate areas to correspond with specific groups. Each group of students works on creating a small mural for a book, making a clearly separated composite of a number of books.

| The Very Quiet Cricket | The Grouchy Ladybug | The Mixed-Up Chameleon |
| The Very Hungry Catepillar | Have You Seen My Cat? | 1,2,3 to the Zoo |

Gigantic Gameboard

Your students may also wish to form groups to make a gigantic board game for their culminating mural. On this board game would be spaces with Eric Carle characters, directions for movement, questions about books that have been studied, or anything else the student groups decide. Of course, the background for the board game would be filled with vibrant color and texture!

The Mural *(cont.)*

Directions:

Review the Eric Carle books you have read in class and ask children to select several of their favorites to include in their mural.

Prepare background paper.

- White paper will best allow the vibrant colors of the tissue paper to be dominant.

- The background can be texture painted, giving an effect that is not flat.

- Object printing with sponges, bottle caps, blocks, fruit, vegetables, and other shape-making objects adds interest to the display.

- Large expanses can be covered by patting crumpled, paint-dipped cloth to the background. This technique is especially effective for sky, sea, and big areas of dirt or grass.

Design the mural. Children should block out their ideas on practice paper first. Be sure to approve their mural designs before they begin to go into "production."

Remind students to protect their clothing with smocks or paintshirts, the floor and furniture with newspaper, and watch where they are walking! Remember to allow plenty of time for clean-up.

Patterns to Use

When making your mural, you may find that you would like to include trees. Here are some suggestions:

- Pine trees can be made easily by texturizing paper for the trunk and needles. For the trunk, use a texturized piece of brown paper or strips of tissue. For the needles, texturize paper with different colors of green paint or tissue, cut strips for needles, and build the tree by gluing the strips to the trunk.

- Other trees can be built upon the same kind of trunk, but branches and leaves should be added. Here are a few leaf patterns to try.

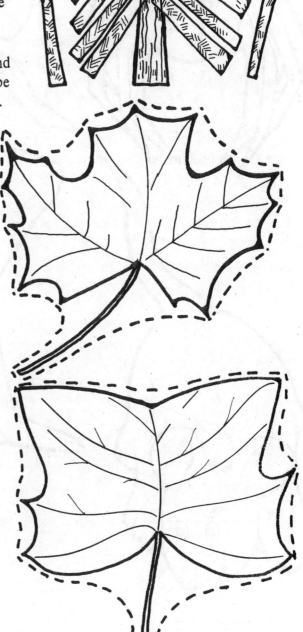

Patterns to Use

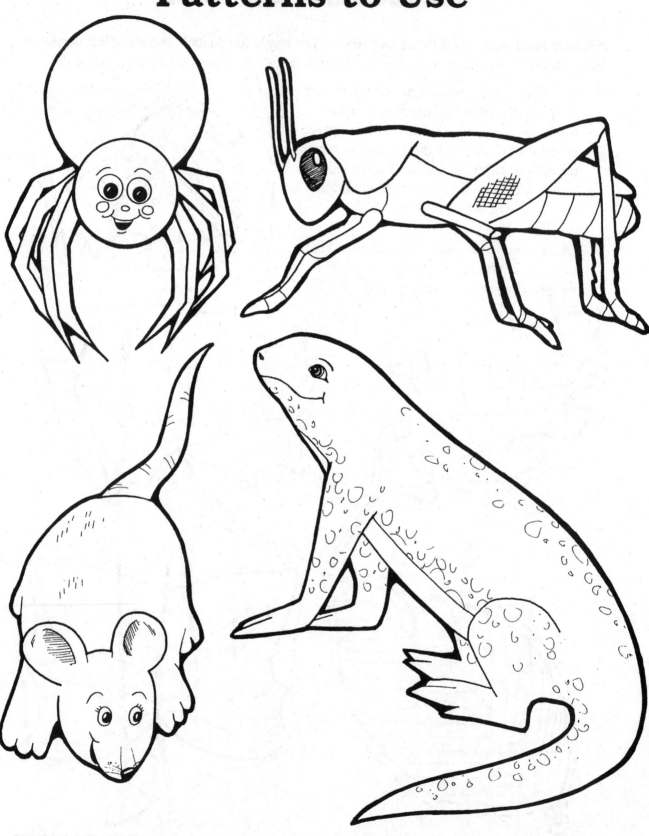

Patterns to Use

Ask each child to cut out a figure and personalize it by adding details and his or her name. Then, invite your students to attach their figures on their favorite part of the mural, or the part to which they contributed.

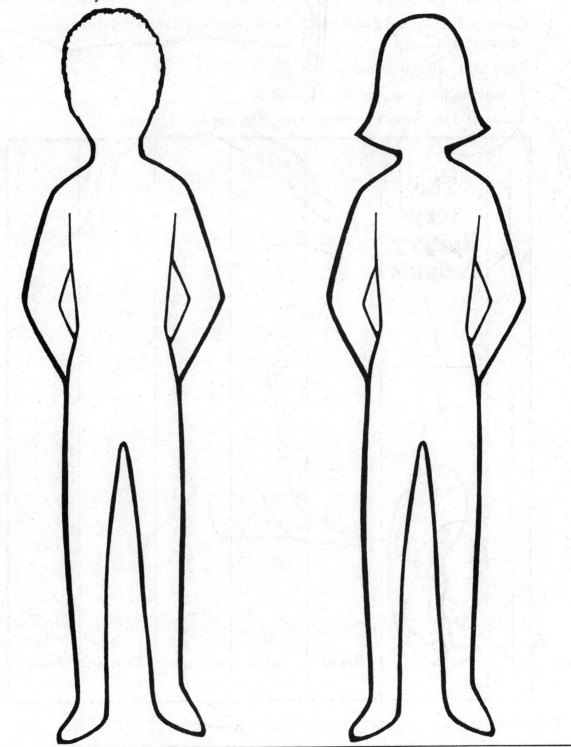

Eric Carle Books

These books make great group projects. Each group member can be responsible for illustrating one page of the group book.

- Cut pages of graduated sizes. (See finished book below.)
- Choose a character and decide what your character will do on several days or at different times.
- Write any text that is necessary.
- Illustrate each page in the style of Eric Carle.
- Remember to save space on the left margin for stapling or binding.

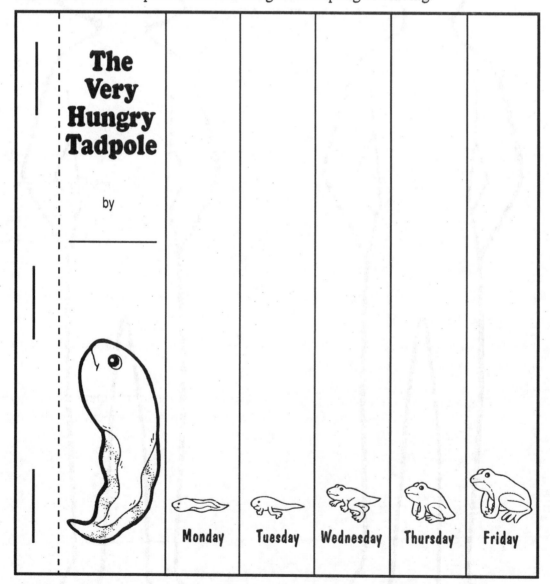

These books can be displayed around your Eric Carle mural!

Introduction to Assessments

Knowledge: *This level of assessment provides students with an opportunity to recall fundamental facts and information about the story.*

Comprehension: *This level of assessment provides students with an opportunity to demonstrate a basic understanding of the story.*

Application: *This level of assessment provides students with an opportunity to use information about or from the story in a new way.*

Analysis: *This level of assessment provides students with an opportunity to examine a part of the story or the style of the author carefully in order to better understand it.*

Synthesis: *This level of assessment provides students with an opportunity to put parts from the story together in a new way to form a new idea or product.*

Evaluation: *This level of assessment provides students with an opportunity to form and present an opinion backed up by sound reasoning.*

Knowledge

Here are a few ideas you can adapt to any of Eric Carle's books your students have studied.

- Ask student volunteers to draw 2 inch by 2 inch black line pictures of the main characters in the story. Collect their pictures and use them to construct a test that requires students to match characters' names with their pictures.

- Supply students with a piece of graph paper and ask them to create a wordsearch or crossword puzzle using the characters in the story.

- Extract quotations from the story and ask the students to match the quotations with the characters who said them.

- Prepare, or have the students prepare, pictures of some of the main events in the story. They will then arrange scrambled story pictures in sequential order.

- Prepare sentences that reflect the main ideas or events in the story. Your students will then arrange scrambled story sentences in sequential order.

- Ask students to create a "Wanted Poster" for one of the main characters.

- Provide students with a sheet of drawing paper on which they are to recall details about the setting by creating a picture of where a part of the story took place.

- Ask students to retell the story!

About the Story

Choose one of these task cards and do what the card asks you to do.

Look at this page from the story. In words or pictures, tell what comes just before it.	Turn to page _____. In your own words, tell what the idea on this page means.
Here is a quote from the story. Why was this said?	If there was one more page in this book, what do you think would be on it?
Look at this page from the story. In words or pictures, tell what comes just after it.	What does this story mean to you?
Explain how the main character felt at the beginning, middle, and end of the story.	What is a question you have about this story?

Teacher: Adapt these task cards for specific books.

Design a Lesson Plan

It is now your turn to apply what you know about what your class likes to do when studying a book. Use the Eric Carle book, *The Very Busy Spider*. Design a "lesson plan" for teaching the book to your classmates!

The Very Busy Spider

by _____

publisher _____

copyright date _____

Summary:

_____

_____

_____

Before Reading the Book:

idea: _____

_____

_____

While Reading the Book:

idea: _____

_____

_____

After Reading the Book:

idea: _____

_____

_____

It's now time to teach your lesson. Have fun!

Which Could Be Eric Carle?

Which one of these drawings looks most like Eric Carle might have done it? Write his name below the drawing you choose. Color the flowers.

You're the Author

Read the words written on the new leaves of this plant. Choose one of the ideas and do it.

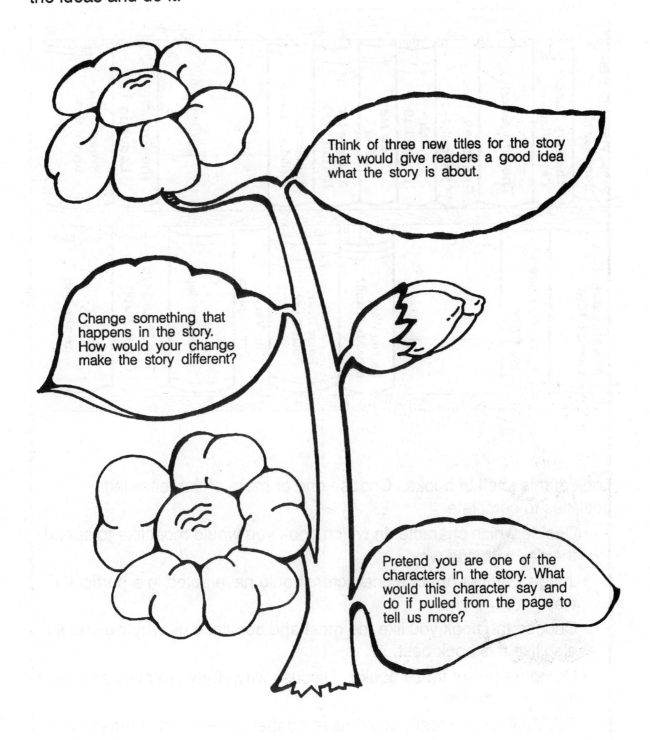

Think of three new titles for the story that would give readers a good idea what the story is about.

Change something that happens in the story. How would your change make the story different?

Pretend you are one of the characters in the story. What would this character say and do if pulled from the page to tell us more?

Think About It

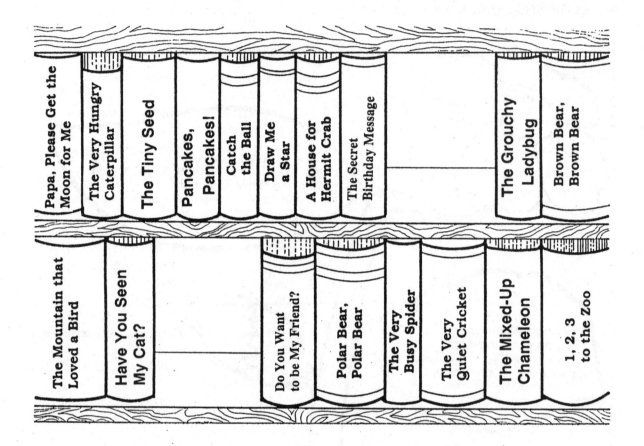

Look at this shelf of books. Choose one or more of the following activities to complete.

- Decide which character in which book you would most like to spend the day with and why.
- Judge whether or not a character should have acted in a particular way.
- Choose the book you like the most and convince us why we should also like this book best.
- Compare two of these books. Discuss ways they are alike and ways they are different.
- Decide if a story really could have happened and justify reasons for your decision.

Bibliography

In addition to the books referred to in this publication, Eric Carle has written and/or illustrated a wealth of other books you will want to include in your Eric Carle library! Here is a partial listing of his works.

Written and Illustrated by Eric Carle:

All Around Us (Picture Book Studio, 1986)

Catch the Ball (Philomel, 1982)

Draw Me a Star (Philomel, 1992)

Eric Carle's Treasury of Classic Stories for Children (Orchard Books, 1988)

The Honeybee and the Robber: A Moving Picture Book (Philomel, 1981)

A House for Hermit Crab (Picture Book Studio, 1988)

I See a Song (Crowell, 1973)

Let's Paint a Rainbow (Philomel, 1982)

My Very First Library Series (Crowell)
  My Very First Book of Colors, 1974
  My Very First Book of Numbers, 1974
  My Very First Book of Shapes, 1974
  My Very First Book of Words, 1974
  My Very First Book of Food, 1986
  My Very First Book of Growth, 1986
  My Very First Book of Heads and Tails, 1986
  My Very First Book of Homes, 1986
  My Very First Book of Motion, 1986
  My Very First Book of Sounds, 1986
  My Very First Book of Tools, 1986
  My Very First Book of Touch, 1986

Rooster's Off to See the World (Picture Book Studio, 1987)

The Very Busy Spider (Philomel, 1984)

Walter the Baker (Knopf, 1972)

What's for Lunch? (Philomel, 1982)

Illustrated by Eric Carle:

Baumann, Hans. *Chip Has Many Brothers* (Philomel, 1985)

Buckley, Richard. *The Foolish Tortoise* (Picture Book Studio, 1985)

Buckley, Richard. *The Greedy Python* (Picture Book Studio, 1985)

Juster, Norton. *Otter Nonsense* (Philomel, 1982)

Knowlton, William. *The Boastful Fisherman* (Knopf, 1970)

Martin, Bill Jr. *Polar Bear, Polar Bear, What Do You Hear?* (Henry Holt and Company, 1991)

Mendoza, George. *The Scarecrow Clock* (Holt, Rinehart & Winston, 1971)

Mitsumasa Anno. *All in a Day* (Dowaya, Tokyo, 1989)

Singer, Isaac Bashevis. *Why Noah Chose the Dove* (Farrar Strauss and Giroux, 1974)

Sundgaard, Arnold. *The Lamb and the Butterfly* (Orchard, 1988)

Whipple, Laura, editor. *Animals, Animals* (Philomel, 1989)

Resources

Carle, Eric, "From Hungry Caterpillars to Bad Tempered Ladybirds," *Books for Your Children* (Spring, 1978)

Carle, Eric, *Something about the Author Autobiography Series,* Volume 6 (Gale, 1988)

"Eric Carle's Children's Books Are to Touch, to Experience, and Most of All to Love," *Early Years,* (April, 1982)

Famous Children's Authors, edited by Shirley Norby and Gregory Ryan (Denison, 1988)

Answer Key

Page 32

Caterpillars in the Classroom

Spring is a good time of year to bring caterpillars into the classroom to observe life cycle stages. Silkworms are especially interesting as they can be kept in a low-sided container and easily observed. They grow rapidly, while voraciously munching on mulberry leaves, and spin white, fibrous cocoons. If caterpillars are difficult to find in your area, they can be obtained through scientific supply houses, such as this:

Insect Lore Products

P.O. Box 1535   Phone: (805) 746-6047
132 South Beech Street   Order Line: 800- LIVE BUG
Shafter, California 93263   FAX Orders: (805) 746-0334

Pages 41-43

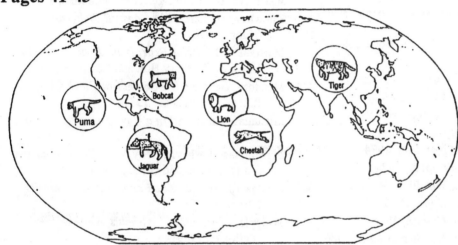

These are the common areas for these animals. Accept any answers that students can support.

Page 46

Answers will vary but should include food (seeds, insects, worms, fish, rodents, etc.), water, nesting materials, and a safe place to build a nest.

Page 58

In this sequencing activity, either the nestled seed or the flower bursting with seeds that begin to fly away can be first.

Page 93

In this pre-reading exercise, you may want to use the survey questions as an oral exercise to generate interest and understanding in self-awareness. Some student responses might need explanatory comments, others will not. For example, when a student answers "Has there ever been a time when many others could do something you could not do?" with a "yes" response, give that student the chance to explain that he or she never thought that the bicycle without training wheels could be conquered.

Page 96

Here is a correctly labeled cricket.

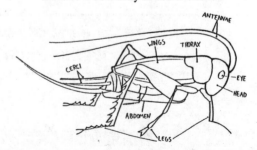
